GREEK
Myths

Acknowledgements

Help with various aspects of this book has been received from many friends and colleagues. For the photographs I am indebted to all those in museums abroad who responded to my requests, and to Christi Graham and P. E. Nicholls of the British Museum Photographic Service. Sue Goddard and Sue Bird produced the map and Sue Goddard and Michael Strand the line drawings, and Brian Cook, Emma Cox, Lesley Fitton and Susan Woodford were kind enough to read early drafts of the text. I am most grateful to them for their helpful comments, especially Susan Woodford, who tactfully mingled encouragement with painstaking and enlightening correction of numerous embarrassing errors of fact and judgement; I am of course solely responsible for those that remain. Finally, without the practical assistance and moral support of my husband, Roger Bland, this book would not have been written, and it is dedicated to him, with affectionate thanks.

Author's Note

It would have been impossible to include the entire corpus of Greek mythology in a book of this size. The myths selected for discussion are of course a personal choice, but they do include some of the most important and interesting; those who feel the need for more may refer to the suggestions for further reading on p. 79. It may be felt that references to the ancient sources are uneven in their occurrence: where it has seemed useful and appropriate, the ancient sources have been closely and extensively followed, but in cases where the sources are numerous, contradictory, late and of little intrinsic interest, it has not seemed desirable to detract from the story by close reference to texts. The same motive, that of putting the myths themselves across as clearly as possible, lies behind the obvious inconsistencies in the transliteration of Greek names. In general, Greek forms have been preferred, so that Herakles and Antaios are used rather than Heracles and Antacus, but where an accurate transliteration might appear strange and jarring, familiar 'English' forms have been used, so that Oedipus and Circe replace the more 'Greek' versions of Oidipous and Kirke.

GREEK Myths

LUCILLA BURN

Orient BlackSwan

ORIENT BLACKSWAN PRIVATE LIMITED

Registered Office
3-6-752 Himayatnagar, Hyderabad 500 029 (A.P.), India
Email: centraloffice@orientblackswan.com

Other Offices
Bangalore, Bhopal, Bhubaneshwar, Chandigarh, Chennai
Ernakulam, Guwahati, Hyderabad, Jaipur
Kolkata, Lucknow, Mumbai, New Delhi, Noida, Patna, Pune

Published by The British Museum Press
A division of The British Museum Company Ltd
38 Russell Square, London WC1B 3QQ

First published 1990
Fourteenth impression 2006

Published in India by
Orient Blackswan Private Limited 2010

ISBN 978 81 250 3947 1

Printed in India at
Aegean Offset Printers
Greater Noida

Published by
Orient Blackswan Private Limited
1/24 Asaf Ali Road, New Delhi 110 002
Email: delhi@orientblackswan.com

Designed by Gill Mouqué
Cover design by Slatter-Anderson

FRONT COVER: *Odysseus and the Sirens, from the Athenian red-figured stamnos (wine jar), about 460 BC.*

THIS PAGE: *A view of Knossos on Crete*
(Photo J. L. Fittton).

Contents

The Greek World

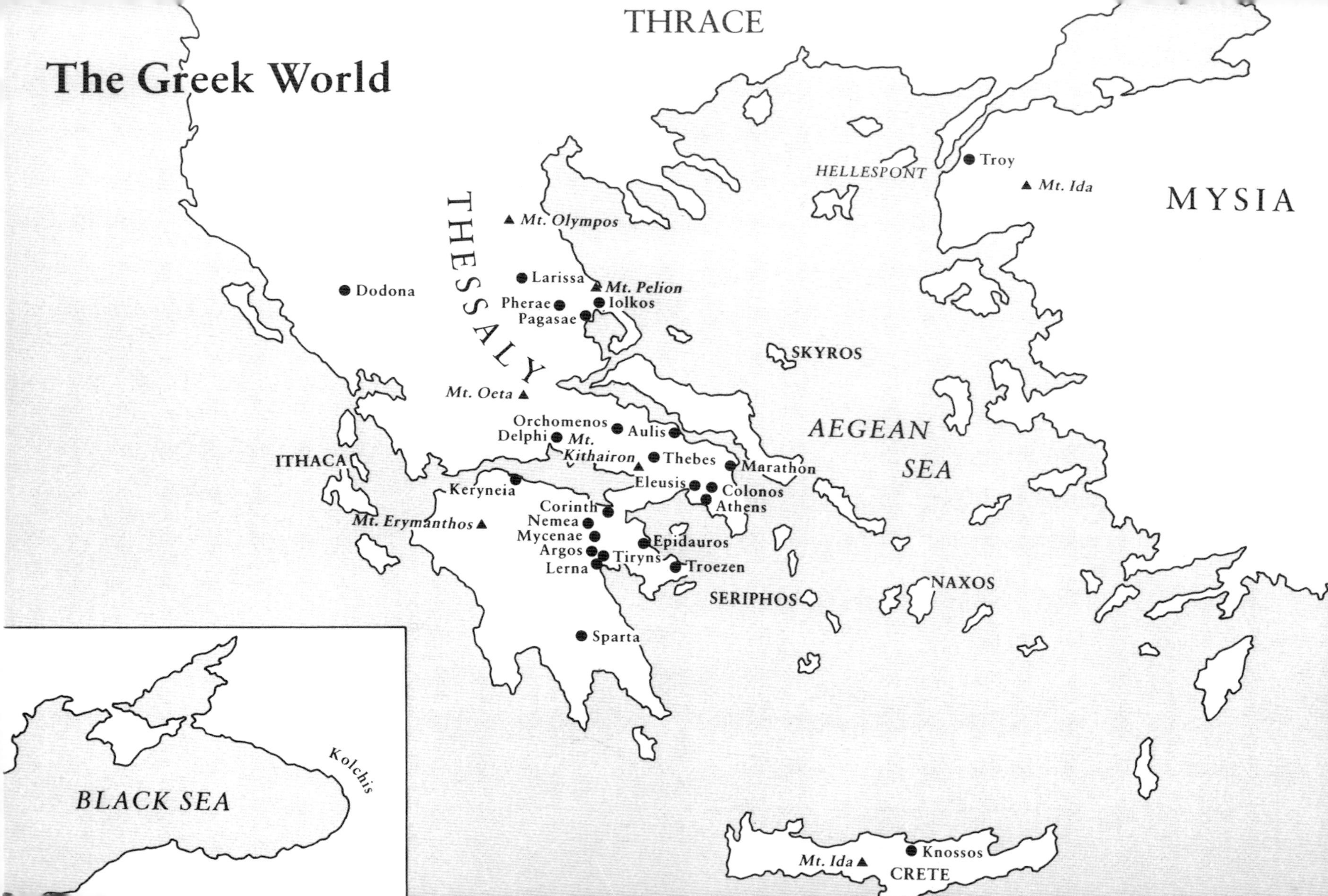

Introduction

Persephone, daughter of Demeter the goddess of grain, was with the daughters of Ocean in a grassy meadow picking flowers. There were roses, lilies, saffron plants, violets, irises and hyacinths, but most beautiful of all, according to the Homeric *Hymn to Demeter*, was a narcissus,

> a trap planted for the blossoming maiden by Earth in accord with Zeus's plans ... it was radiantly wonderful, inspiring awe in all who saw it, whether immortal god or mortal man; a hundred stems grew from its root; and the whole wide heaven above, the whole earth, and the salt surge of the sea smiled for joy at its fragrance.

As Persephone reached out to the irresistible flower, the earth fell from under her feet, and out from the chasm rushed the chariot of Hades, king of the Underworld and brother of Persephone's father Zeus. He snatched up Persephone and, despite her cries and screams, carried her off to his underground kingdom to be his wife. Only one goddess, Hekate, heard her, and only the sun-god Helios saw the rape; but as Persephone passed out of the light, the mountains and the rocks sent back echoes of her cries to her mother Demeter.

Distraught with grief and worry, Demeter cast a veil over her head and for nine days searched the earth for her daughter, never stopping to rest or even eat. Then Helios told her what had happened and that it was the will of Zeus for Persephone to marry her uncle. Demeter's grief was now mingled with fury; leaving Mount Olympos and the other gods, she wandered in disguise over the earth among mortal men until she arrived at Eleusis. There, in the house of Keleos, she became nursemaid to Keleos's infant son Demophon. She tried to make Demophon immortal by placing him at night in the flames of the fire. One night his mother stayed awake to watch, but when she saw her son in the hearth she cried out in terror and the wrathful Demeter was provoked to reveal her true identity. The people of Eleusis built a temple for the goddess and there she remained, totally neglecting her duties, and mourning for her lovely daughter:

> She made the most terrible, most oppressive year for men upon the nourishing land, and the earth sent up no seed, as fair-garlanded Demeter hid it. Cattle drew the many curved ploughs in vain over the fields, and much white barley seed fell useless on the earth ...

Eventually Zeus, king of all the gods, took notice and summoned Demeter to his presence. But she utterly refused to return to Olympos, or to allow the crops to grow, until she saw her daughter again. So Zeus sent his messenger

Hermes to fetch Persephone home. The cunning Hades obeyed his brother's command to release Persephone into the upper world, but before he let her go he made her eat a pomegranate seed, which meant that she would have to return to him again. Persephone was therefore only temporarily reunited with Demeter and Zeus ordained that she should spend two-thirds of the year above ground with her mother and one-third in the misty darkness as the wife of Hades.

Demeter had to be content with this arrangement. Now, as she sped over the earth, the barley sprang up and ripened below her feet. Returning to Eleusis, she explained to the leaders of the people the rites that were to be performed there in her honour and in honour of Persephone. These rites were to be the Eleusinian Mysteries, whose contents were a closely kept secret: all the *Hymn to Demeter* will reveal of them is that

> Blessed of earthbound men is he who has seen these things, but he who dies without fulfilling the holy things, and he who is without a share of them, has no claim ever on such blessings, even when departed down to the mouldy darkness.

Myths have recently been defined as 'traditional tales relevant to society', and although this definition may seem a little colourless, its two propositions clearly do apply to the myth of Demeter and Persephone. Like most other Greek myths, it is so 'traditional' that it is scarcely possible to say when it arose. The *Hymn to Demeter* is the earliest extant version of the story, and in its present form it is generally thought to date to the seventh century BC. But like the slightly earlier epic poems, the *Iliad* and the *Odyssey*, the *Hymn* probably existed for several centuries before this in the form of oral poetry handed down through the generations. Very few Greek myths appear to have been invented in historical times: the vast majority seem as old as Greek civilisation itself.

The myth of Demeter and Persephone is also highly 'relevant to society'. Not only is the division of Persephone's year between the upper and the under worlds a vivid image of the division of the year into its different seasons; the myth also encompasses some of the most fundamental issues of human existence. In the first place it is concerned with the provision of food, necessary to sustain life. In the Greek world the most basic food was bread. When Demeter ceases to look after the crops and the grain fails to grow, man faces starvation. The Eleusinian Mysteries, it is thought, were in part concerned with propitiating Demeter in order to ensure the fruitfulness of the fields. But at the same time the myth of Persephone is an allegory of the natural social requirements for girls to grow up and leave home. In the end Demeter does not get her daughter back on a permanent basis, for Persephone must be reconciled with fulfilling her function as a wife. In Greek literature of the fifth century and later it is clear that the rape of Persephone is seen as the paradigm for all weddings; all girls weep as they are dragged from their mothers' sides, and again and again the imagery of marriage is that of rape and death. Like Persephone's descent to the world of the dead, from which

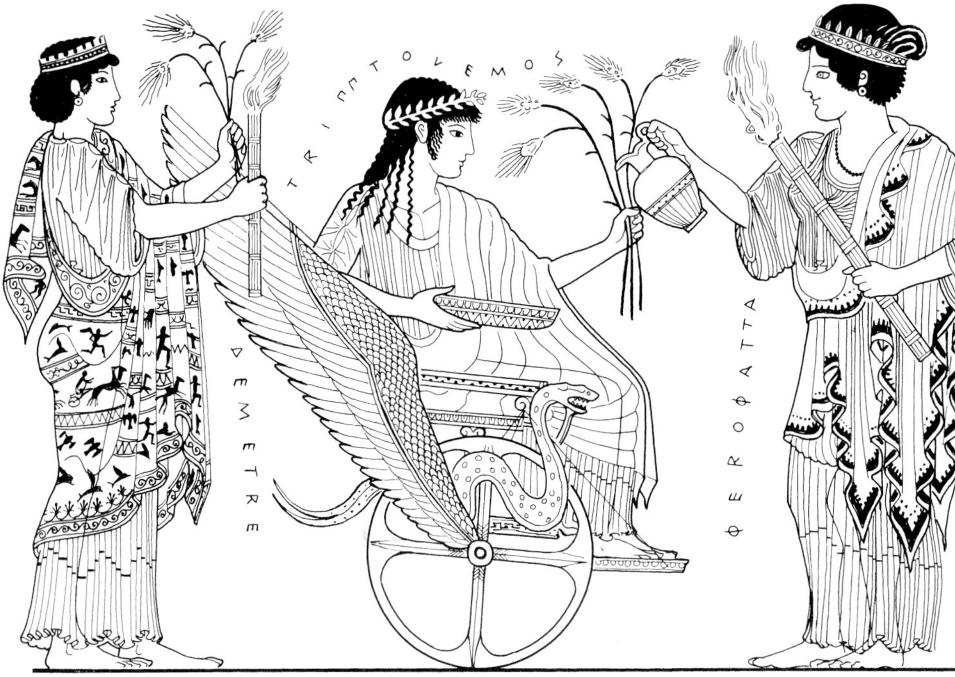

Demeter *(left), goddess of the harvest, often holds stalks of wheat or barley; the torches she and her daughter* **Persephone** *both hold suggest their connections with the Underworld. Here they are sending the hero Triptolemos to take the gift of corn to mankind.*

she emerges as a wife, Greek marriage was a rite of passage, involving a girl's separation from her own family, her initiation into the duties of a wife, then her reintegration into society, where she may again mix with her own relations, but with a different status.

Greek myths permeated Greek life, private and public. In the well-documented society of Athens in the fifth century BC, for example, it is clear that a major part of education was learning and reciting epic poems on heroic subjects. Guests at drinking parties might entertain each other by reciting stories from myths, or they might listen to a professional performer, who would sing of the deeds of heroes while accompanying himself on the lyre. Private homes contained pottery vessels decorated with scenes from the adventures of the gods and heroes; these same vessels accompanied their owners to the grave. Scenes of myth could also be woven into fine textiles.

Moving outside the home, most of the great public religious festivals were linked with specific mythological incidents, and these were commemorated in the rites which marked such occasions. At the spring festival of the Anthesteria, for instance, there was both a re-enactment of the sacred marriage of Dionysos and Ariadne and a silent drinking competition which commemorated the occasion on which Orestes, polluted by matricide, sought sanctuary at Athens. To comply with the laws of hospitality and yet avoid contaminating anyone who shared a table with him, Orestes was put to sit on his own, and he ate and drank in silence. At the Anthesteria, therefore, each participant in the drinking contest sat silently at his own table and drank from his own jug. The Homeric *Hymn to Demeter*, interweaving its mythological narrative with allusions to the great Mysteries of Eleusis, provides another typical example of the way Greek myth and cult were inextricably blended.

Greek myths inspired great art and great poetry. The large-scale mythological paintings which decorated the walls of such important fifth-century Athenian buildings as the Theseion (the Shrine of Theseus) do not survive, and we are left to imagine from ancient descriptions how impressive they must have been; occasional survivals, such as the painting of the Rape of Persephone in a fourth-century tomb at Vergina in Macedonia, are a tantalising reminder of what we have lost. Much more architectural sculpture survives from all periods of Greek art. In the sculptured metopes of the Parthenon, for example, we can see episodes from the battle between men and centaurs; the sculptural programme of the Great Altar at Pergamon in Asia Minor, built in the second century BC to honour the gods and glorify a ruling dynasty, provides not only an extremely vivid representation of the battle between gods and giants, but also a rare and invaluable record of a lesser myth, that of the local hero Telephos. Not just for painters and sculptors, but for poets too, the great corpus of Greek myths was their basic raw material and source of inspiration. Each year at the great dramatic festivals of classical Athens, versions of the familiar myths, either freshly worked or in popular old revivals, were brought before the public; and at the festivals of the gods hymns of praise and commemoration, both new and old, were sung; the *Hymn to Demeter* may well have been composed for such an occasion. Were it not for the remarkable poetic qualities of these reworkings of the old stories, and the lasting appeal of their beauty, both our present knowledge of Greek myths and their fascination would be far less.

The principal characters of the *Hymn to Demeter* are gods and goddesses, but in most Greek myths heroes (and heroines) play a more prominent part. The Greeks of the historical period liked to think that the Age of the Heroes had preceded their own times. As the poet Hesiod explained in the late eighth century BC, Zeus, the king of the gods, had created five successive races of men. The race of Gold had been the first to inhabit the earth: these fortunate people had lived a carefree existence like the gods, with the earth producing food for them of its own accord. They were succeeded by an inferior Silver race of people weak in both body and mind; and in their turn the men of Silver were replaced by those of Bronze. The men of Bronze lived principally for war; they were great and terrible warriors, and in time they destroyed themselves entirely.

To replace them Zeus created a new and glorious breed, 'a godlike race of heroes, who are called demi-gods – the race before our own'. These were the men whose deeds and characters inform Greek myth: they routed fabulous monsters, crossed the sea in search of Helen, died on the plain of Troy or ringed the seven-gated citadel of Thebes; after death they enjoyed a god-like existence in the Islands of the Blessed at the ends of the earth. To the fifth and last race of men the pessimistic Hesiod himself belonged. His was the race of Iron, in which unceasing work was relieved only by death: 'I wish I were not of this race, that I had died before, or had not yet been born.' Hesiod's feelings were echoed by many later Greeks, who looked back with regretful nostalgia to the lost Age of the Heroes as a not far-distant time when life had been both more noble and more glorious.

Nobility and glory were fundamental to the Greek concept of the hero. While many heroes had a divine father or mother – the father of Herakles was Zeus and the sea-nymph Thetis was the mother of Achilles – all were of noble birth; they were kings or princes, rulers of countries or cities, commanders of armies, possessors of fabulous wealth. They were invariably good-looking, athletic and brave. They adhered to strict standards of behaviour: they were respectful towards women and others in need of protection – the laws of hospitality, for example, were sacred, and no hero worthy of the name would drive a beggar from his hearth. Most important, however, was the heroes' obsession with fame and glory. Like the knights of medieval chivalry they rose eagerly to every challenge, whether it were the sacking of a city or the slaying of a Minotaur.

The world of the heroes was not distinctly segregated from that of the gods; the gods came and went among them, helping their sons or particular favourites and laying traps for those with whom they were displeased. Both gods and heroes, however, were subject to the higher authority of fate. Again and again we come across characters who are aware of their destiny, like Achilles and his parents, who knew that if Achilles went to Troy he would die there. Fate might be revealed through oracles, such as that of Apollo at Delphi, or through such intermediary agents as prophets, dreams and omens. But very often heroes had only a partial understanding of what was fated, and their inability to recognise and accept their destiny might well lead to tragedy, as in the case of Oedipus.

In the chapters which follow we shall be more concerned with heroes than with gods, but the gods are always present in the background: their relationships, passions, jealousies and spheres of influence and responsibility formed the backcloth against which the heroes played out their dramas. Before looking at the myths themselves, therefore, we will first look briefly at the gods.

The principal gods of the Greeks are often referred to as 'the twelve Olympians', after their home on Mount Olympos. There were actually at least thirteen important deities and numerous lesser figures besides. Chief among the gods was **Zeus**, whose grandfather was **Uranos**, personification of the sky; Uranos lay over **Gaia**, the earth, and she produced countless children, the youngest of whom was **Kronos**. Growing weary of child-bearing, Gaia enlisted the aid of Kronos, who cut off his father's genitals with a sickle and threw them into the sea. Kronos went on to marry his own sister **Rhea**, but since he knew that he in his turn was destined to be overthrown by

***Poseidon** (below), the sea-god, generally bears a trident; here he is riding on a hippocamp, a creature part fish and part horse.*
***Hera** (right), like Aphrodite, has no special attributes beyond her sceptre and her beauty.*

one of his own sons, he swallowed his first three daughters and two sons as soon as each was born. When she was pregnant with Zeus, Rhea escaped to Crete and gave birth in a cave on Mount Ida. Leaving the infant there in the care of the nymphs, she returned to Kronos and presented him with a large stone wrapped up in swaddling clothes, which he duly swallowed, thinking it was his newborn child. When Zeus grew up, he forced his father to regurgitate all his older brothers and sisters; they then declared war on Kronos, overcame him and confined him forever in the depths of Tartarus, below the surface of the earth.

Next, Zeus and his brothers drew lots to determine how their power should be divided. **Poseidon** was given control of the seas and **Hades** power

***Aphrodite**, goddess of love, is here shown riding on one of her sacred birds, the goose. She has no special attributes beyond her beauty, but her association with the fertility of nature may be suggested as here by flowers or tendrils of vegetation.*

over the underworld and the dead, while Zeus won overall sovereignty, ruling over the earth and the sky. Their three sisters were **Hestia**, goddess of the hearth, **Demeter**, goddess of crops and grain, and **Hera**, wife of Zeus.

These six were the older generation of the Olympians, but many of the children of Zeus became equally important. Some were born to Hera, the rest to a variety of mothers. Hera gave birth to **Ares**, the god of war, and the lame smith-god **Hephaistos**, as well as **Hebe**, goddess of youth, and **Eileithyia**, goddess of childbirth. There are differing accounts of the parentage of **Aphrodite**, the goddess of love: either she was the daughter of Zeus and Dione, or else she was born from the foam which arose when Kronos threw the genitals of Uranos into the sea. **Athena**, goddess of wisdom and of war, was the daughter of Zeus and **Metis**, the personification of counsel; her birth was unusual, for when Metis was already pregnant, Zeus learnt of a prophecy that if she gave birth to a daughter, she would go on to produce a son who would rule the universe. So Zeus swallowed Metis, and in due course Athena sprang fully grown and fully armed from her father's head, helpfully split open by Hephaistos. The daughter of Zeus and Demeter was, as we have

***Zeus**, leader of the gods, is always bearded and often brandishes a thunderbolt, as here. The smith-god **Hephaistos** (right) usually wears a short tunic, as here, and he may carry an axe. Here he has just used the axe to split open Zeus's head, from which emerges **Athena**, goddess of wisdom and of war, brandishing her shield.*

***Apollo** (left) usually plays the lyre; his sister **Artemis** is generally armed with a bow and quiver, and frequently accompanied by wild animals.*

seen, **Persephone**, goddess of the Underworld. Leto bore Zeus the twins **Apollo**, the god of music and poetry, and **Artemis** the huntress; Semele bore **Dionysos**, god of wine; and Maia was the mother of **Hermes**, the messenger god.

It is not possible here even to attempt to answer the question of how the Greeks saw their gods. Undoubtedly they regarded them in different ways at different times, their views changing with the progress of their civilisation, and the development of their scientific knowledge and moral philosophies. For the present it must suffice to take the gods as we find them in the myths. In the Homeric poems, for example, the gods are at their most anthropomorphic, resembling nothing so much as a large, powerful, talented and extremely quarrelsome human family. The story of Ares and Aphrodite, as recounted in the *Odyssey*, serves as a useful example of their behaviour and may conclude this introduction.

The beautiful Aphrodite, goddess of love, was married to Hephaistos, god of fire and metal-working, but conceived a passion for Ares, god of war. Hephaistos, though a consummate smith and craftsman, was lame and ugly, while Ares was handsome and virile. Aphrodite and her lover used to meet secretly in Hephaistos's palace, until one day the Sun saw them and told the smith-god what was going on. Hephaistos was furious, and immediately contrived a wonderful net, light as gossamer but strong as iron, invisible to the naked eye; this he fastened around Aphrodite's bed before departing on a well-publicised trip to the island of Lemnos. Ares was quick to seize the opportunity and went straight to Aphrodite. But as the pair lay entwined in each other's arms, the net fell around them and caught them up so that they could not move. Hephaistos, warned again by the Sun, hurried home and gave vent to his rage; standing in the doorway he shouted to all the other gods to come and look at the shameless couple. Poseidon, Apollo and Hermes all turned up, though the goddesses stayed modestly at home. When they saw Hephaistos's clever trick, 'a fit of uncontrollable laughter seized these happy gods'; there were suggestions that Ares would have to pay Hephaistos the fine paid to husbands by adulterers, and Apollo asked Hermes if he would care to take Ares's place; Hermes replied that even if the chains were three times as strong and even if all the gods and goddesses were looking on, he wouldn't give up such a chance of sleeping at Aphrodite's side. The respectable Poseidon, however, was rather embarrassed by the affair and urged Hephaistos to set them free. Eventually, when Poseidon offered to guarantee any recompense that Ares promised to pay, Hephaistos relented and released the chains. The luckless pair fled in disgrace, Ares to Thrace and the discomfited Aphrodite to her sanctuary of Paphos in Cyprus, where the Graces bathed and anointed her and dressed her in fine clothing, so that she was once more a marvel to behold.

Dionysos *(left), the wine-god, wears a wreath of vine or ivy leaves in his hair; here he carries a spray of vine leaves in his hand.*

Hermes *(right), messenger of the gods, wears winged boots to speed him over land and sea; he usually has a petasos, the broad-brimmed travellers' hat, and he carries a caduceus, a special form of staff.*

The labours of Herakles

Herakles, the greatest of all the Greek heroes, was the son of Zeus and Alkmene. Alkmene was the virtuous wife of Amphitryon, and in order to seduce her Zeus assumed the form of Amphitryon while the latter was absent from home. When her husband returned and found out what had happened, he was so angry that he built a great pyre and would have burnt Alkmene alive, had Zeus not sent the clouds to extinguish the flames and so forced Amphitryon to accept the situation. Once born, the infant Herakles was quick to reveal his heroic potential. While still in his cradle, he strangled two snakes which Zeus's jealous wife Hera had sent to attack him and his half-brother Iphikles; while still a boy, he killed a savage lion on Mount Kithairon. In adult life the adventures of Herakles were both more extensive and more spectacular than those of any other hero. Throughout antiquity he was hugely popular, the subject of numerous stories and countless works of art. Although the most coherent literary sources for his exploits date only from the third century BC, scattered references and the evidence of the artistic sources make it very clear that most if not all of his adventures were well known from the earliest times.

Herakles performed his famous twelve labours at the command of Eurystheus, king of Argos or Mycenae. There are several explanations as to why Herakles found himself obliged to carry out all Eurystheus's tiresome and seemingly impossible requests. One source suggests that the labours were a penance imposed upon the hero by the Delphic oracle when, in a fit of madness, he had killed all the children of his first marriage. While the first six labours are all set in the Peloponnese, the later labours took Herakles to various places on the fringes of the Greek world and beyond. Throughout the labours Herakles was pursued by the hatred of the goddess Hera, who was always jealous of Zeus's children by other women. The goddess Athena, on the other hand, was an enthusiastic supporter of Herakles; he also enjoyed the company and occasional assistance of his nephew, Iolaos.

The first labour of Herakles was the killing of the Nemean Lion. Since this enormous beast was invulnerable to any weapon, Herakles wrestled with it and eventually choked it to death with his bare hands. Afterwards he removed the skin with the aid of one of its claws, and wore it ever after as a cloak, with the paws knotted round his neck, the jaws gaping above his head and the tail swinging out behind. The second labour required the destruction of the Lernaean Hydra, a many-headed water-snake which was

Alkmene on the pyre *Alkmene, the mother of Herakles, sits on a pyre built of logs, her right hand raised imploring mercy; her husband Amphitryon holds torches to the pyre, but Zeus sends two Clouds who pour water on to the flames and so save Alkmene's (and Herakles's) life. Paestan red-figured bell-krater (wine-bowl), about 330* BC.

Herakles and the Hydra *Neither Herakles, nor the winged Athena who accompanies him, appear to have noticed the Hydra coiled behind the goddess, three forked tongues hissing from three ferocious mouths. Etruscan bronze mirror, fifth century* BC.

Herakles and the Boar *Herakles offers the Boar to Eurystheus, who cowers terrified inside a large storage-jar partly sunk in the ground. Herakles wields the huge animal as though it weighs nothing. Athenian black-figured amphora (wine-jar), about 530 BC.*

Herakles and the Stymphalian Birds *(opposite) The beautifully patterned and coloured birds fly or perch before Herakles, their wings and long necks stretched in a variety of graceful attitudes. Herakles takes aim with his sling. Athenian black-figured amphora (wine-jar), about 530 BC.*

plaguing the swamps around Lerna. Every time Herakles cut off a head, two more grew in its place, and as if this were not bad enough, Hera sent a giant crab to nip Herakles in the foot. This mean trick was too much for the hero, who decided to enlist the aid of Iolaos; while Herakles cut off the heads, Iolaos cauterised the stumps with a blazing torch so that no more could grow, and finally they got the better of the monster. Afterwards Herakles dipped his arrows in the Hydra's blood or venom and so made them poisonous.

On Mount Erymanthos, a fierce wild boar was rampaging and laying waste the countryside. Eurystheus rather rashly asked Herakles to bring it back to him alive, but the ancient illustrations of this episode, which mostly show the cowardly Eurystheus taking refuge in a storage jar, suggest that he came to regret his request. It took Herakles a whole year to accomplish his next labour, which was to capture the Keryneian Hind. This animal seems to have been more shy than dangerous. It was sacred to the goddess Artemis, and, though female, possessed most wonderful antlers. According to the legend, when Herakles had finally caught the Hind and was taking it to Eurystheus, he encountered Artemis, who was most displeased and threatened to kill Herakles for his impudence in capturing her animal; but when she learned about the labours, she agreed to let Herakles take the Hind on condition that Eurystheus released it as soon as he had seen it.

The Stymphalian Birds were so numerous that they were destroying all the crops in the neighbourhood of Lake Stymphalos in Arcadia; various sources claim that they were man-eating, or at the very least able to shoot their feathers out like arrows. It is not altogether clear how Herakles met the challenge: one vase painter shows him attacking with a sling, but other sources suggest he shot them with arrows from his bow or scared them away with a bronze rattle specially made for the job by the god Hephaistos. The

last of the six Peloponnesian labours was the cleansing of the Augean Stables. King Augeias of Elis owned vast herds of cattle, whose stables had never been cleared out, so that the dung was several metres deep. Eurystheus must have thought that the task of cleansing the stables in a single day really would prove impossible, but Herakles once more rose to the occasion, diverting the course of a river so that its waters did the whole job for him.

Eurystheus now asked Herakles to capture the wild, ferocious Cretan Bull, the first labour to take him outside the Peloponnese. Once Eurystheus had seen it, Herakles released the Bull, and it survived to be killed by Theseus at Marathon. Next, Eurystheus sent Herakles to Thrace to bring back the man-eating horses of Diomedes. Herakles tamed these animals by feeding them their brutal master, and brought them safely home to Eurystheus. He was immediately sent off again, this time to the shores of the Black Sea, to fetch the girdle of the queen of the Amazons. Herakles took an army with him on this occasion, but he would not have needed it if Hera had not stirred up trouble. When he arrived at the Amazon city of Themiskyra, the Amazon queen was quite happy for him to take her girdle; Hera, feeling this was too easy, started a rumour that Herakles was trying to carry off the queen herself, and a bloody battle ensued. Herakles did of course escape with the girdle, but only after heavy fighting and much loss of life.

In order to accomplish his last three labours, Herakles passed entirely beyond the boundaries of the Greek world. First he was sent beyond the edge of the Ocean, to distant Erytheia in the farthest west, to fetch the Cattle

Herakles and the Horses of Diomedes *Herakles stands nonchalantly between the two rearing horses, one hand on the neck of each. Etruscan bronze group, fourth or third century BC.*

Herakles and the Bull *The prancing Bull is not totally subdued; the hero braces his body against the Bull's flanks, both hands restraining its head. Roman ivory group, first or second century AD.*

Herakles and Geryon *The herdsman and the savage dog having been dealt with, Herakles here turns his attention to Geryon himself. One of the three heads falls back, perhaps already wounded. Athenian black-figured amphora (wine-jar), about 540 BC.*

of Geryon. Geryon was a formidable challenge; not only was he triple-bodied, but to help him guard his wonderful red cattle he also employed a ferocious herdsman named Eurytion and a two-headed, snake-tailed dog named Orthos. Orthos was the brother of Cerberus, the dog who guarded the entrance to the Underworld, and Herakles's encounter with Geryon is sometimes interpreted as his first meeting with death. Although Herakles disposed of Eurytion and Orthos without too much difficulty, Geryon, with his three fully armed bodies, proved a more formidable adversary, and only after a terrible struggle did Herakles succeed in slaying him. When he arrived back in Greece, Eurystheus sent him out on a still more desperate errand, to descend to the Underworld and fetch Cerberus, the hound of Hell himself. Guided by the messenger-god Hermes, Herakles descended to the gloomy realm of the dead, and with the consent of Hades and Persephone he borrowed the fearsome, triple-headed monster to show to the terrified Eurystheus; this done, he politely returned the dog to its rightful owners.

Even then Eurystheus demanded one last labour: that Herakles should bring him the Golden Apples of the Hesperides. These apples, the source of the gods' eternal youth, grew in a garden at the end of the earth; they had been a wedding present from Gaia, the Earth, to Zeus and Hera. The tree which bore the golden fruit was tended by nymphs called Hesperides and guarded by a serpent. Accounts vary as to how Herakles tackled this final labour. Those sources which locate the garden below the Atlas Mountains, where the mighty Atlas held up the sky on his shoulders, say that

Herakles and Cerberus *(left) Eurystheus takes cover in his storage-jar again, as Herakles lets Cerberus bound forward to greet him, snakes hissing from his three mouths and writhing around his six front paws. Caeretan hydria (water-jar), about 520 BC.*

Herakles in the Garden of the Hesperides *(below) Herakles rests at the end of his final labour. The Hesperides prepare to hand over their apples, while the guardian snake coils languidly around his tree. Athenian red-figured hydria (water-jar), about 420–400 BC.*

Herakles persuaded Atlas to fetch the apples for him; while he went off on this errand, Herakles shouldered the sky himself, and when Atlas returned Herakles had some difficulty in persuading him to resume his burden. Other versions of the story suggest that Herakles went to the garden himself and either fought and killed the serpent or else persuaded the Hesperides to hand the apples over to him. The apples of the Hesperides symbolised immortality, and this final labour meant that eventually Herakles would ascend to Olympos and take his place among the gods.

In addition to the twelve labours, many other heroic deeds and adventures were ascribed to Herakles. In his quest for the garden of the Hesperides, he had to wrestle with the sea-god Nereus to compel the god to give him

Herakles and Busiris *(below) Having escaped sacrifice at the hands of the Egyptian king, Herakles sets about punishing his oppressors. One Egyptian is about to be battered to death by Herakles's club; the others flee, scattering musical instruments and implements of sacrifice. Athenian red-figured kylix (drinking-cup), about 520–500 BC.*

Herakles and the Delphic tripod *(below right) Herakles and Apollo, the god of Delphi, enact a tug of war over the Delphic tripod. Apollo's sacred animal, the deer, appears to be pulling on his side. Athenian red-figured calyx-krater (wine-bowl), about 500–480 BC.*

Herakles and Antaios *(above) Herakles lifts the giant Antaios away from the Earth, his mother Gaia, in order to deprive him of his source of strength. Bronze coin of the Roman Emperor Antoninus Pius, AD 142–3.*

the directions he required; on another occasion he confronted another marine deity, Triton. Traditionally it was in Libya that Herakles encountered the giant Antaios: Antaios was a son of Gaia, the Earth, and he was invulnerable so long as he retained physical contact with his mother. Herakles wrestled with him and lifted him off his feet; deprived of maternal support, he became quite powerless in the hero's mighty arms. In Egypt Herakles had a narrow escape from sacrifice at the hands of King Busiris. A seer had once advised Busiris that sacrificing foreigners was a sure method of alleviating droughts. Since the seer was himself a Cypriot, he became the first victim of his own advice; when the method proved gratifyingly effective, Busiris ruled that all foreigners misguided enough to enter his kingdom should be sacrificed. When it was Herakles's turn, he let himself be bound and led to the place of sacrifice before turning the tables on his assailants and butchering the lot of them.

Herakles was not infrequently involved in conflicts with the gods. On one occasion, when he failed to receive a response he had hoped for from the Delphic priestess, he tried to make off with the sacred tripod, saying he would found a better oracle of his own. When Apollo tried to stop him, a fierce quarrel broke out, which was only resolved when Zeus hurled a thunderbolt between them.

Herakles was very loyal to his friends; more than once he risked his own life to help them, most spectacularly in the case of Alkestis. Admetus, king of Pherae in Thessaly, had made an arrangement with Apollo that when the time came for him to die, he would be allowed to live on provided that he found someone else who was willing to die in his place. However, when Admetus was later on the verge of death, it proved harder than he had anticipated to find a substitute; after his elderly parents had selfishly refused to sacrifice themselves, his wife Alkestis insisted that she should be the one to die. When Herakles arrived she had already descended to the Underworld, and he instantly set off after her. He then wrestled with Death and won, bringing her back in triumph to the world of the living.

Herakles was the Greek Superman, and many of the stories of his deeds are simply gripping tales of superhuman achievements and fabulous monsters. At the same time Herakles, like Odysseus, stands for the average man, and his adventures are exaggerated parables of human experience. Quick-tempered, not terribly bright, fond of wine, food and women (his amorous adventures are too numerous to detail here), he was an eminently sympathetic figure; and on the whole his example was to be emulated, for he destroyed evil and championed good, rising above all the blows that fortune showered on him. Above all, he offered some hope of defeating man's ultimate and crucial challenge, death.

Herakles's end was characteristically dramatic. Once, when he and his new bride Deianeira were crossing a river, the centaur Nessos offered to carry Deianeira over, and in midstream tried to rape her. Herakles shot him dead with one of his poisonous arrows, and as he expired, Nessos, simulating repentance, urged Deianeira to take some of the blood from his wound and keep it safe; if Herakles ever seemed to be tiring of her, she should soak a garment in the blood and give it to him to wear; after that he would never look at another woman. Years later Deianeira remembered this advice when Herakles, on his way home from a distant campaign, sent on ahead of him a beautiful captive princess with whom he was evidently in love. Deianeira sent her husband a robe dyed in the blood; as he put it on, the poison of the Hydra ate into his skin and he collapsed in frightful agony. His eldest son Hyllos took him to Mount Oeta and laid his mangled but still breathing body on a funeral pyre, which was eventually kindled by the hero Philoktetes. However, the labours of Herakles had ensured his immortality, and so he ascended to Olympos and took his place among the gods who live for ever.

Theseus of Athens

Theseus was the quintessential Athenian hero, the embodiment of all that the Athenians thought was best and most distinctive about themselves. He was endowed with most of the same superhuman characteristics as Herakles, and his deeds were almost as impressive. But he was more refined and civilised than Herakles, a consummate statesman who could number among his achievements not merely the establishment of such religious and social institutions as the great Panathenaic festival of Athens, but also the political consolidation of Attica and the foundation of the Athenian democracy.

Theseus's mother was Aithra, the daughter of Pittheus, king of Troezen in the Argolid. His father was either Aigeus, king of Athens, or the sea-god Poseidon; Aigeus was thought to be sterile, and Aithra had lain with both on the night that Theseus was conceived. Aigeus was worried that his nephews, the fifty sons of Pallas, would try to murder their cousin if they knew of his existence, and so the boy was brought up at Troezen by his mother and grandfather. Beneath a great rock at Troezen, Aigeus concealed a sword and a pair of sandals, giving instructions that when Theseus was strong enough to lift the rock, he should be allowed to travel to Athens in search of his father. When Theseus had passed this test, his mother told him that it was time for him to set out for Athens. However, both she and Pittheus were most anxious that Theseus should not go by land, for the road from Troezen to Athens lay across the isthmus of Corinth, which was plagued by villains and ruffians of all description. But Theseus was determined not to avoid the danger; he hoped to emulate the deeds of Herakles and win renown by overcoming the hazards of the road.

The deeds accomplished by Theseus on his journey from Troezen to Athens seem to have been designed to rival those of Herakles. They were almost certainly the subject of an epic poem, which no longer survives. Tradition says that Theseus met his first challenge at Epidauros, where he came upon Periphetes, a lame brigand who wielded a huge, knotted club; Theseus wrested it from him, killed his opponent and took the weapon along to help in the rest of his adventures. All the way across the isthmus Theseus played the brigands at their own murderous games and won.

His second adversary, Sinis, specialised in tearing travellers limb from limb: he would bend two pine trees to the ground, tie one arm and one leg of his victim to the top of one tree and the other arm and leg to another,

Theseus lifting the rock *Watched by his mother Aithra, Theseus exerts all his strength to push away the huge rock and reveal the sword and sandals left there by his father. In a variation on the usual story, there is a quiver with the other objects. Roman terracotta relief ('Campana plaque'), first century* BC *or* AD.

then let go of the trees so that they sprang up and tore the wretched man apart. When Theseus drew near, Sinis asked him to test his strength by helping him to bend down a pine tree. Theseus agreed, but cunningly ensured that it was he rather than Sinis who first let go of the tree, and Sinis rather than he who ended up flying through the air. Surveying the sad remains of earlier travellers suspended around him, Theseus then bent down two trees and tied Sinis between them, so that he met the same painful death he had enjoyed inflicting on others. Theseus next encountered the Krommyonian Sow, a fierce wild pig which was ravaging the land; this creature too he killed.

The bandit Skiron had positioned himself where the isthmus was at its narrowest, with a sheer drop down to the sea on either side of the road. As Theseus approached, Skiron commanded him to kneel down and wash his feet. Theseus warily obeyed, kneeling as far from the edge as he could. As he did so, Skiron shouted that he should go and feed Skiron's turtle and tried to kick him over the cliff. But Theseus was too quick for him, and Skiron ended up in the sea. At Eleusis, the wrestler Kerkyon challenged Theseus to a bout, but he too found that he had met his match.

Drawing nearer to Athens, Theseus was urged by the infamous Prokrustes to spend the night on his wonderful bed, a couch guaranteed to provide the perfect fit for all comers. Prokrustes would invite travellers to lie down and then set to work to make them fit the bed: if they were too short, he pounded them with a mallet in order to stretch them out, and if they were too long, he lopped off their feet and heads. Theseus was to be Prokrustes's last visitor, and Prokrustes's own mutilated body was the final occupant of his terrible bed.

When Theseus finally arrived at Athens, he found his father Aigeus under the spell of the sorceress Medea, who had promised to cure him of his supposed sterility and give him numerous sons. Theseus did not reveal his identity to Aigeus, but Medea knew at once who he was. Since his arrival on the scene had rather spoiled her plans, she tried hard to get him out of the way. First she suggested to Aigeus that he should ask the young stranger, who claimed to have dealt with so many villains, to get rid of the Bull of Marathon; brought from Crete by Herakles, this creature was then ravaging the Athenian countryside. Despite its enormous size and the fire it breathed from its nostrils, Theseus managed to subdue the beast and bring it back to Athens, where he sacrificed it to the city's patron goddess, Athena.

Foiled in her first attempt to get rid of Theseus, Medea now tried to poison him. According to tradition, her attempt took place at the public banquet which accompanied the sacrifice of the Bull of Marathon. Just as Medea set a cup of poison on the table, Theseus drew the sword he had brought with him from Troezen as though to cut the meat of the sacrifice. Aigeus, recognising the weapon, sprang up in surprise and delight and upset the cup, whose contents spilt over the floor, hissing and eating their way into the marble. Father and son were reunited, and the discredited Medea was forced to flee for her life.

Theseus proceeded to get rid of the challenge to his father and himself from his cousins, the sons of Pallas, whom he ambushed and completely routed. But now there was another ordeal he had to face – the Minotaur. Every nine years Minos, king of Crete, demanded from Athens a tribute of seven girls and seven youths, whose fate was to be sacrificed to the beast. The Minotaur, a monstrous creature with the body of a man and the head of a bull, was the child of Minos's wife Pasiphae and a bull sent from the sea by Poseidon. Its home was the Labyrinth, a dark maze of endlessly winding corridors, blocked exits and confusing turns, built for Minos by the master-craftsman Daidalos.

The legend of the human tribute may reflect an era when the Minoan civilisation exercised control over Athens, but the Theseus story refers to a more specific incident: Aigeus had earlier sent Minos's son Androgeos to fight the Bull of Marathon, and he had been killed, so it was in compensation for his death that the tribute was exacted. At any rate, soon after the defeat of the sons of Pallas, the time for the tribute approached, and when Theseus found out about it, he was determined to be one of the party. Aigeus was overcome by grief, and tried hard to dissuade him, but Theseus would not change his mind, promising Aigeus that he would slay the Minotaur and return safely home.

Aigeus was convinced that he would never see his son again. However, he made sure that the ship which carried the youths and girls to Crete was equipped with two sets of sails, one black and the other white. They set sail with the black ones, as suited the melancholy nature of the expedition, but Aigeus requested that if they returned in triumph they should hoist the white set as a signal he could see from the Acropolis. Upon the ship's arrival in Crete the Athenian party was hospitably entertained by Minos and the Cretan court; during a display of athletics Minos's daughter Ariadne saw and fell instantly in love with Theseus. When the time came for the victims to enter the Labyrinth, Theseus, who had asked to go first, was secretly supplied with a ball of thread by Ariadne; he made one end fast to a point near the entrance and unwound the ball as he travelled through the maze. Finally he came to the centre and found himself face to face with the Minotaur,

The deeds of Theseus *In the centre, Theseus drags the defeated Minotaur from the Labyrinth, suggested by the meander-and-chequer border. Round about, Theseus is shown with Sinis, the Krommyonian Sow, the wrestler Kerkyon, Prokrustes, Skiron, and the Bull of Marathon. Athenian red-figured kylix (drinking-cup), about* 440–420 BC.

The Centauromachy *The Centaur gropes at a wound in his back, his powerful torso arched in pain; the youthful Lapith arrests his adversary with his left hand, lifting his right to deliver a decisive blow. The two figures strain away from each other, but are formally reunited by the backcloth of the Lapith's heavy cloak. Marble metope (relief panel) from the Parthenon, Athens, 445–440 BC.*

a far more terrifying creature than any he had before encountered. Theseus had no weapon, but with his bare hands he fought off the monster's attack and eventually wore down its strength to the point where he was able to break its neck. Thoroughly exhausted but unharmed, with the aid of the thread he retraced his steps to the exit, where Ariadne was anxiously awaiting him. Together they collected the rest of the Athenians, fled to their ship and instantly set sail for the mainland.

For neither Theseus nor Ariadne did the story have an entirely happy ending. Ariadne had made Theseus promise to take her with him back to Greece, but he abandoned her on the island of Naxos, in circumstances not altogether clear. The popular and romantic version of the story is that the gods made Theseus forget all about Ariadne, so that he left her sleeping in a secluded spot where she was later discovered by Dionysos. However, more prosaic sources, anxious to explain and excuse such unheroic conduct on the part of Theseus, suggest that he put her ashore on Naxos because she was pregnant and badly seasick; then he and his ship were swept out to sea by a storm and she was left to die in labour. In this version of the story, Theseus had the black sails hoisted on the ship as he approached Athens because he was still mourning the loss of Ariadne; the more usual account is that in his eagerness to return home he simply did not remember to change them for the white ones. So Aigeus, anxiously scanning the horizon, was greeted by the sight of the black sails; believing that his son had perished, he threw himself to his death from the rocks of the Acropolis.

After the death of Aigeus, Theseus became king of Athens, but his involvement in heroic adventures did not cease. Invited to the wedding of his close friend Peirithoos, king of the Lapiths, Theseus found himself in the thick of a great battle with the centaurs, creatures part-man and part-horse.

Peirithoos had invited the centaurs to his wedding feast because they were his neighbours, but they had drunk too much wine and tried to carry off the Lapith women, including the bride. Only with heavy losses did Theseus and the others manage to beat off the attack.

Theseus was frequently involved in amorous affairs. His abduction of the Amazon Antiope led to the Amazon invasion of Attica, only repulsed after fierce fighting. In their old age Theseus and Peirithoos joined forces to abduct two daughters of Zeus, Helen and Persephone. They managed to kidnap Helen (this was before she became the wife of Menelaos), but when they descended to the Underworld in search of Persephone things started to go badly wrong. Persephone's consort Hades, god of the Underworld, invited the pair to sit down to a meal with him; when they tried to rise, they found they were stuck to their seats. Eventually Herakles managed to rescue Theseus, but Peirithoos was compelled to remain in the Underworld forever. Theseus's own death was strangely unheroic: he was pushed over a cliff on the island of Skyros by Lykomedes, its king.

The principal source for the story of Theseus is Plutarch, a Greek philosopher, priest and moralist who lived in the later first and earlier second centuries AD. Amongst his works is a series of parallel *Lives* of various famous Greeks and Romans, some historical, others legendary. In the *Lives* Theseus is paired with Romulus, an indication of the political significance which tradition attached to him: if Romulus was the founder of Rome, Theseus was the father of Athenian democracy. This idea seems to have originated in the last years of the sixth century BC, when democratic reforms were initiated by the Athenian statesman Kleisthenes. Many reforms are ascribed both to Theseus and to Kleisthenes; both are said to have organised the unification of Attica and to have divided the people into the three classes which were to be the basis of the political divisions of Athens in the historical period. Theseus, like Kleisthenes, is held to have established various civil and judicial councils and assemblies; to have founded festivals; and to have initiated such economic reforms as the minting of coins. It is thought that a new epic poem on the subject of Theseus may have been commissioned by Kleisthenes or by the new democracy, and it is certainly true that from the late sixth to the mid-fifth century, the popularity of Theseus rivals that of Herakles in Athenian art and thought. He appears on the sculptural decoration of temples and on the painted vases which people used in daily life and took with them to the grave. In 490 BC, when the Athenians were hard pressed by the Persians at the Battle of Marathon, it was Theseus, founder of the way of life which they were fighting to preserve, who was said to have appeared at the head of the army and inspired the soldiers with new strength.

Around 475–470 BC huge bones were found in a tomb on Skyros; they were identified as belonging to Theseus and ceremonially brought home to Athens, where a special shrine, the Theseion, was built to house them. At this time Theseus was not merely a figure of mythology for the Athenians, but a political symbol too, the image of their democracy.

The Trojan War

Did the Trojan War take place? The extent of the appeal which the story of Troy has exercised over successive generations is demonstrated by the efforts of countless historians, archaeologists and romantic enthusiasts to establish the historical basis of the Trojan War and to discover the site of Troy. Today it is generally agreed that the site was correctly identified in the late nineteenth century by Heinrich Schliemann as the mound of Hissarlik on the plain by the Dardanelles, on the north-west coast of Turkey. However, Schliemann's claim to have discovered the Troy of the Trojan War is now largely discredited. The mound of Hissarlik contains numerous successive habitation levels, and it was in one of the earliest that Schliemann claimed to have discovered wonderful treasure: this settlement is now thought to be about a thousand years too early to have been destroyed by Greeks from the Mycenaean palaces of the Greek mainland. They might, though, have been instrumental in the destruction of one of the later settlements of Hissarlik, which seems to have been burnt to the ground, possibly after a siege, at about the right time (around 1200 BC). This later Troy was a relatively humble settlement, but in its destruction may lie the kernel of historical reality around which the legend grew. However, the development of the legend remains a mystery unlikely to be solved by archaeology, and so there is no danger that the romantic enigma of Troy will ever be destroyed.

Whatever its basis in historical fact, the Trojan War is the single most important episode, or complex of episodes, to have survived from Greek mythology and legend. The events which led up to the actual war and those which followed are combined in the group of stories known as the Trojan Cycle; some are known from the two great Homeric poems, the *Iliad* and the *Odyssey*, but other sections of the story have to be pieced together from numerous later sources, ranging from the Greek tragedians of the fifth century BC to much later Roman authors. The story as a whole may be compared to a Wagnerian opera in the richness and complexity of its interweaving of characters and themes; it is hugely romantic and of great human appeal, for like all Greek myths it is fundamentally the story of man and of his struggle to exist in the face of fate and the gods.

One of the first links in the chain of events which formed the prelude to the Trojan War was forged by Prometheus, the great benefactor of mankind. Prometheus, a cousin of Zeus, had given man fire, an element whose benefits had previously been enjoyed solely by the gods. He had also instructed men

Peleus and Thetis *(right) Peleus grasps Thetis firmly in a wrestling hold. The panther on Peleus's back and the wolf-head with snake attachments to the right of Thetis's head suggest her transformations into a variety of animals in her attempt to make Peleus release his hold. Athenian black-figured amphora (wine-jar), about 500* BC.

The Judgement of Paris *(below) As Hera and Athena approach from the left, Paris turns to the Eros at his shoulder and looks across at Aphrodite, seated on the right. Hermes stands between her and Paris. Emerging from behind a hillock above him is Eris, personification of Strife and a presentiment of the abduction of Helen and the ten-year struggle for Troy. Athenian red-figured hydria (water-jar), about 420–400* BC.

to offer to the gods only the fat and bones of meat sacrifices, and to keep the best bits for themselves. To punish Prometheus, Zeus chained him to a rock high in the mountains and daily sent an eagle to eat his liver, which grew again by night.

According to some sources, Prometheus was eventually set free by Herakles, but others state that he was released by Zeus when he finally agreed to tell him an important secret. This secret concerned the sea-nymph Thetis, who was so beautiful that she counted several gods among her suitors, including Poseidon and Zeus himself; however, a prophecy known only to Prometheus foretold that the son of Thetis was destined to be greater than his father. On learning this, Zeus rapidly abandoned the idea of fathering a son by Thetis himself, and decided that she should marry the mortal Peleus instead; their son would be Achilles, the greatest of the Greek heroes at Troy.

Thetis at first resisted the advances of Peleus, changing into fire, serpents, monsters and other forms, but he held tightly on to her through all her transformations and eventually she had to submit. All the gods and goddesses of Olympos save one were invited to the magnificent wedding of Peleus and Thetis; and in the middle of the feast Eris (Strife), the only goddess who had been left out, burst in and threw among the guests the apple of discord, inscribed (though we hear of this only from very late sources) 'for the fairest'. This apple was claimed by three goddesses, Hera, Athena and Aphrodite. Because they were unable to reach an agreement, and Zeus was understandably reluctant to decide the issue himself, he sent the goddesses to have their beauty judged by the herdsman Paris on Mount Ida, outside the city of Troy on the eastern shore of the Mediterranean.

Paris was a son of Priam, king of Troy, but when Priam's wife Hecuba was pregnant with him, she dreamed she was giving birth to a torch from which streamed hissing serpents, so when the baby was born, he was handed over to a servant with orders to take him out to Mount Ida and kill him. The servant, however, instead of killing him, simply left him on the mountain to die; he was rescued by shepherds or herdsmen, and brought up to be one himself. As Paris was minding his flocks on the mountain, Hermes led the three goddesses to him for judgement. Each offered him a reward if he would choose her; Hera wealth and power, Athena military prowess and wisdom, and Aphrodite the love of the most beautiful woman in the world. Awarding victory to Aphrodite, he incurred the undying wrath of the other two, who became henceforward implacable enemies of Troy. Shortly afterwards Paris returned by chance to Troy, where his prowess in athletic contests and his amazingly handsome appearance aroused the interest of his parents, who soon established his identity and received him back with rapture.

The most beautiful woman in the world was Helen, the daughter of Zeus and Leda. Many kings and noblemen had wished to marry her, and before her mortal father, Tyndareus, announced the name of the successful suitor, he made them all swear an oath to abide by Helen's choice and to come to the aid of her husband if she should ever be abducted. Helen married

Menelaos, king of Sparta, and by the time that Paris came to visit them they had a daughter, Hermione. Menelaos welcomed Paris into his home, but Paris repaid his hospitality by stealing Helen and escaping with her back to Troy. Helen's part in this was explained in different ways by various sources: either she was abducted against her will, or Aphrodite drove her mad with desire for Paris, or, most elaborate of all, she never went to Troy at all, and it was for the sake of a phantom that the Greeks spent ten long years at war.

The expedition sets sail

Menelaos summoned all Helen's former suitors, and all the other kings and noblemen of Greece, to help him mount an expedition against Troy to recover his wife. The leader of the Greek force was Agamemnon, king of Mycenae and elder brother of Menelaos. The Greek heroes came from all over the mainland and the islands to the port of Aulis, the assembly point from which they planned to sail across the Aegean to Troy. Their origins and the names of their leaders are listed in the great Catalogue of Ships near the beginning of the *Iliad*:

> The tribes (of warriors) came out like the countless flocks of birds – cranes or long-necked swans – that gather in the Asian meadow by the streams of Cayster, and wheel about with harsh cries as they come to ground on an advancing front. So tribe after tribe streamed out from the ships and huts . . . innumerable as the leaves and flowers in their season.

Some of the heroes came to Aulis more willingly than others. Odysseus, king of Ithaca, knew it had been prophesied that if he went to Troy he would not return for twenty years, and so he feigned madness when the herald Palamedes came to summon him, yoking two mules to a plough and driving them up and down the beach; but his ploy was revealed when Palamedes put Odysseus's infant son Telemachos in the way of the mules, and Odysseus immediately reined in his team. Achilles's parents, Peleus and Thetis, were reluctant to let their young son join the expedition, since they knew it was fated that if he went he would die at Troy. In an attempt to evade his destiny they sent him to Skyros, where, disguised as a girl, he mingled with the daughters of the king, Lykomedes. During his stay he married one of the daughters, Deidameia, who bore him a son, Neoptolemos.

Odysseus, however, discovered that the Greeks would never capture Troy without the assistance of Achilles, and so he went to Skyros to fetch him. According to one version of the story, Odysseus disguised himself as a pedlar, gained entrance to the court and spread out his wares before the women; among the jewels and textiles were weapons in which the young Achilles displayed a revealing interest. Another source describes how Odysseus arranged for the sound of a trumpet to be heard in the women's quarters: while the genuine daughters scattered in confusion, Achilles stood his ground and called for arms. His disguise abandoned, Achilles was easily persuaded to accompany Odysseus back to Aulis, where the fleet was preparing to sail.

The huge Greek force, whose greatest heroes were Agamemnon, Menelaos, Odysseus, Aias, Diomedes and Achilles, was ready to sail, but the wind held stubbornly against them. Eventually the prophet Kalchas revealed that the goddess Artemis demanded the sacrifice of Agamemnon's daughter, Iphigeneia, before the wind could turn. Agamemnon was horrified by this, but public opinion forced him to comply: Iphigeneia, summoned on the pretext that she was to marry Achilles, was instead slain upon the altar. Some sources say that Artemis took pity on her and substituted a deer at the last moment; at all events the wind veered round, and the ships set sail.

The wrath of Achilles

It is sometimes assumed that the *Iliad* is the story of the Trojan War. In fact, although it ranges widely over the whole story, its ostensible subject, as announced in its first lines, is rather more restricted:

> Sing of wrath, goddess, the destructive wrath of Achilles, son of Peleus, that brought countless sorrows to the Achaeans, and sent many valiant souls of heroes to Hades, while their bodies made carrion for dogs and birds, and the will of Zeus was fulfilled...

The story of the *Iliad* is, then, the story of Achilles, and of his quarrel with Agamemnon. At the opening of the *Iliad* the Greeks had already been at Troy for nine years. They had sacked much of the surrounding countryside and skirmished sporadically with any Trojans who had emerged from behind their massive fortifications. The Greeks were wearying of the campaign and irritated by their inability to score a decisive victory over Troy itself, when Achilles fell out with Agamemnon over a matter of honour.

Agamemnon, as his share of the booty from a raid in which Achilles had played the leading part, had been allotted a girl named Chryseis, daughter of Chryses, priest of Apollo. Chryses offered Agamemnon a fine ransom for her release but Agamemnon refused to give her up. So Chryses prayed to Apollo, who sent a plague upon the Greek camp, and the prophet Kalchas revealed that it would be lifted only if Agamemnon gave Chryseis back. Achilles was all in favour of him doing this, but Agamemnon was reluctant. They quarrelled, and Agamemnon eventually agreed to do as he was told, but in order to reassert his authority over Achilles in the most insulting way he could, and simultaneously compensate himself for the loss of Chryseis (whom he claimed to prefer to his own wife Clytemnestra), he took away from Achilles *his* slave-girl, Briseis. Achilles was justifiably enraged. Not only was it an insult to his honour, but it was grossly unfair, as he, Achilles, had done most of the fighting necessary to procure all the treasure and booty that Agamemnon felt he had a right to enjoy. Accordingly, Achilles withdrew to his tent, and took no more part in the fighting or the council meetings. The fighting grew fiercer, with more direct attacks made on Troy and the Trojans. But the Greeks were hard pressed without their greatest fighter, and even Agamemnon was eventually forced to make overtures to Achilles, offering

Odysseus, Diomedes and Dolon *The Greek heroes Odysseus and Diomedes surprise the Trojan spy Dolon in the dark. The painter has treated the subject as a burlesque, with the facial features of the three and their stealthy movements between the trees grotesquely caricatured. Lucanian red-figured calyx-krater (wine-bowl), about 410–400 BC.*

him riches of all description, along with the return of Briseis. Achilles, however, rejected all appeals, declaring that even if Agamemnon's gifts were 'as many as the grains of sand or the particles of dust' he would never be won over.

At this point, Odysseus and Diomedes went out on a night expedition to see what the Trojans were up to. Unknown to them, a Trojan named Dolon was setting out on a similar errand: the Greeks surprised him, and forced him to tell them the dispositions of the Trojan camp. On his recommendation they ended their night excursion with an attack on the encampment of Rhesus, king of Thrace, with whose beautiful horses they escaped back to the Greek camp.

Despite the success of this daring raid, in the overall fighting the Greeks were being driven back to their ships by the Trojans and were in desperate straits, when Achilles's friend Patroklos came to him and begged to be allowed to lead Achilles's troops, the Myrmidons, into battle. He also asked if he could borrow Achilles's armour in order to strike terror into the ranks of the Trojans, who would mistake him for Achilles. Achilles agreed, and Patroklos went out and fought long and gloriously, before, predictably, he was slain by Hector, son of Priam and the best fighter on the Trojan side.

Achilles was overcome by grief. His mother, the sea-nymph Thetis, came to him, and promised him new armour to replace that which had been lost with Patroklos. The new armour, made by the smith-god Hephaistos, included a beautiful shield covered with figured scenes, cities at peace and war, scenes of rural life with flocks, herds and rustic dances, and round the rim of the shield ran the River of Ocean. Achilles and Agamemnon were reconciled, and Achilles returned to the field of battle, where he slaughtered Trojan after Trojan with his spear, 'like a driving wind that whirls the flames this way and that when a conflagration rages in the gullies on a sun-baked mountainside and the high forest is consumed'. After killing many Trojans and surviving even the attack of the River Scamander, which tried to drown him in its mountainous waves, Achilles was at last able to meet his chief adversary, Hector.

The rest of the Trojans had fled from the onslaught of Achilles and taken refuge within their walls, but Hector remained outside the gates, deliberately awaiting the duel which he knew he must fight. Yet when Achilles finally appeared, Hector was overcome by understandable terror and turned to flee. Three times they ran the circuit of the walls of Troy before Hector stopped and bravely faced his great opponent. Achilles's spear lodged in Hector's throat and he fell to the ground. Barely able to speak, Hector begged that Achilles should allow his body to be ransomed after his death, but Achilles, furious with the man who had killed Patroklos, spurned his appeal and proceeded to subject the body to great indignities. First he dragged it by the heels behind his chariot round the walls of the city, for all of Troy to see. Then he took the body back to the Greek camp, where it lay untended in his huts.

Achilles then arranged an elaborate funeral for Patroklos. A huge pyre was built; over it many sheep and cattle were slaughtered and their carcasses

New armour for Achilles *The sea-nymph Thetis and her sisters, riding on dolphins, bring the new armour made by Hephaistos to replace that which was lost with Patroklos. Thetis herself carries a shield, emblazoned with a springing lion. Athenian red-figured and white-ground lekythos (oil-flask), about 440–420* BC.

piled around the body of the dead hero. Jars of honey and oil were added to the pyre, and then four horses and two of Patroklos's dogs. Twelve Trojan prisoners were slaughtered over the pyre, which was then set alight. It burned all night, and all night Achilles poured libations of wine and mourned aloud for Patroklos. The next day the bones of Patroklos were collected and laid in a golden urn, and a great mound was raised where the pyre had been. Funeral games with magnificent prizes were held, with competitions for chariot racing, boxing, wrestling, running, armed fighting, throwing the discus and archery. And every day at dawn, for twelve days, Achilles dragged the body of Hector three times round the mound, until even the gods, who had foreseen and arranged all this, were shocked, and Zeus sent Iris, messenger of the gods, into Troy to visit Priam and instruct him to go secretly to the Greek camp with a fine ransom, which Achilles would accept in return for relinquishing the body of Priam's son.

So Priam, escorted by a single herald, set out for the Greek camp, and was met in the dusk as he drew near to the Greek ships by Hermes, disguised as a follower of Achilles. Hermes guided Priam through the Greek camp, so that he arrived unseen at the hut of Achilles. Priam went straight in and threw himself at Achilles's feet: he asked the hero to think of his own father Peleus, and to show mercy on the father who had lost so many of his fine sons at the hands of the Greeks; he asked to be allowed to take the body of his greatest son back to Troy with him in order that he should be properly mourned and buried by his kinsmen. Achilles was moved by his appeal; they wept together, and Priam's request was granted. So Hector's body was returned to Troy, where he was mourned and buried with appropriate rites.

Here the *Iliad* ends, but it is by no means the end of the story of Troy. The rest of the story is recounted partly in the *Odyssey* and partly by the tragedians, but also by later Roman authors, principally Virgil in the *Aeneid* and a miscellany of later poets such as Quintus of Smyrna. After the death of Hector, a series of allies came to the assistance of the Trojans, including the Amazons under their queen, Penthesileia, and the Ethiopians led by Memnon, a son of Eos, goddess of the dawn. Both Penthesileia and Memnon were killed by Achilles. But Achilles had always known that he himself was fated to die in Troy, far from his native land, and eventually he was killed by an arrow, shot from the bow of Paris. Achilles's mother, Thetis, had wanted to make her son immortal, and when he was a baby she had taken him down into the Underworld and dipped him into the waters of the River Styx; this made his body impervious to injury, except for the heel by which she held him, and it was here that the arrow struck.

The sack of Troy

After the death of their greatest champion, the Greeks resorted to guile in their efforts to capture Troy, which had withstood their siege for ten long years. The Wooden Horse was said to have been the idea of Odysseus, while

The death of Penthesileia *Achilles has forced the Amazon Queen to the ground and, as she looks up at him, he drives his spear into her throat. The brutality of the action is emphasised by the way her face and throat are shown naked and defenceless, while only Achilles's eye is visible through his helmet. According to one tradition, their eyes met in this instant and, belatedly, they fell in love. Athenian black-figured amphora (wine-jar), about 540 BC.*

The Wooden Horse *This is the earliest known representation of the Horse: the artist has given it wheels, and there are port-holes in the sides for the warriors to look out. Some brandish weapons through the port-holes, while others have already emerged from the Horse. Relief pithos (large storage-jar) from Mykonos, 650–600 BC.*

the craftsman responsible for its manufacture was Epeios. When it was built, a party of the boldest Greeks climbed into it, including Odysseus himself and Neoptolemos, son of Achilles. The rest of the Greek force burnt their huts and set sail, but they went only as far as the island of Tenedos, where they beached their ships and waited. The Trojans, scarcely daring to believe that the Greeks had sailed for home, scattered over the plain, marvelling at the Horse and reminding each other of where the Greek camp had been. Soon some shepherds came across a single Greek who had been left behind, Sinon, who told them that his compatriots had wanted to sacrifice him in order to acquire a favourable breeze for their journey; he had with difficulty escaped his chains. This story aroused the compassion of the Trojans, so that they were well disposed to believe the rest of his account. He said that the Greeks, believing that Athena had turned against them, had decided to sail home and attempt to regain the divine favour that their expedition had originally enjoyed. They had made the Horse to propitiate Athena, and they had deliberately made it large in order that the Trojans would not be able to take it within their walls. If the Horse did enter Troy, the city could never be taken; if it stayed outside, the Greeks would definitely return and raze the city to the ground.

A few of the Trojans mistrusted the Horse and were reluctant to bring it within their walls. Priam's prophetic daughter Cassandra, whose fate it was never to have her prophecies believed, warned of the death and destruction its entry into Troy would bring. And Laokoon, the priest of Poseidon, cast his spear against the flanks of the Horse, which resounded with the clang of armed men, and declared that he feared the Greeks, even when they brought gifts. But as he was preparing a sacrifice to the god he served, two great serpents came up from the sea and strangled first his two young sons and then Laokoon himself, before gliding on to take refuge under the altar of Athena. Upon this omen the Trojans hesitated no more, but proceeded to drag the great Horse within their walls, pulling down their fortifications in order to do so. Even then, the hiding place of the Greek heroes might have been discovered, for Helen took it into her head to come down to the Horse, and, walking round it, to call out the names of the Greek heroes, mimicking the voice of each man's wife. Some were tempted to reply, and only Odysseus had the presence of mind to stifle their voices.

When darkness fell, the treacherous Sinon signalled to the fleet at Tenedos, which returned silently to its old anchorage; Sinon also released the heroes from their confinement in the Horse, and the scene was set for the sack of Troy. As the Greeks from the Horse were joined by their comrades from the ships, the Trojans awoke from sleep to find their city going up in flames. The men fought desperately, resolved at least to sell their lives dear, appalled by the sight of their wives and children being dragged from their places of refuge to be either slaughtered or taken prisoner. Most pitiable was the death of Priam, murdered at the altar in his courtyard by Neoptolemos, son of the man who had killed his son Hector. Among the few to escape from Troy was Aeneas, son of Anchises and the goddess Aphrodite. Warned by his mother, he left the city with his little son Ascanios and his elderly father, carrying with him the gods of Troy; his wife followed behind them, but was lost in the confusion, the darkness and the wreckage of the dying city. Aeneas himself was fated after much wandering to reach Italy, where he founded a new and greater Troy, the forerunner of Rome.

The adventures of the Greek heroes on their way home from Troy, and the various homecomings they enjoyed, were enshrined in a number of epic poems known as *Nostoi* (Returns). Of these poems the *Odyssey*, which describes the return of Odysseus to his homeland of Ithaca, is the only one to survive; the returns of the other heroes must be pieced together from a variety of later sources. We shall come to Odysseus shortly, but first we will deal with the homecoming of the leader of the Greeks, Agamemnon, king of Mycenae.

The return of Agamemnon

Agamemnon and Menelaos were the sons of Atreus, who committed a terrible crime when, in a family quarrel, he served his own brother Thyestes with a dish concocted from the severed limbs of Thyestes's children. This act brought a curse upon the house of Atreus, and the fate which met Agamemnon on his return from Troy was in part just retribution for his father's original crime. In Agamemnon's ten-year absence from Mycenae, the government was in the hands of his wife Clytemnestra, assisted by her lover Aigisthos, the one surviving child of Thyestes. A chain of beacons lit against the sky had relayed the news of the great victory at Troy back to mainland Greece, and by the time Agamemnon arrived at his palace, Clytemnestra's plans were well advanced.

Meeting her husband in front of the entrance, she insisted that he should trample over the purple textiles she spread out before him, in a triumphal entrance into his hall. Agamemnon was reluctant to commit such an act of insolence and impiety, but eventually he gave in, and so ensured his doom. Following him indoors, Clytemnestra attacked him as he lay defenceless in the bath, first ensnaring him in a net, before murdering him most brutally with an axe. Her motives for this savage killing were complex, but it would seem that it was not so much her guilty passion for Aigisthos and her desire to see him avenged for the wrong done to his father and brothers, as her hatred of Agamemnon that drove her to his murder. He had brutally murdered her first husband and child before her eyes; he had sacrificed their daughter Iphigeneia at Aulis. She wanted vengeance.

The curse of Atreus did not die with Agamemnon, for he and Clytemnestra had two more children eager to avenge their father's death, Orestes and Elektra. Orestes, when a baby, had been sent away from Mycenae to the safety of Phokis by his sister, anxious to preserve him from their scheming mother. Elektra herself remained at home and was very badly treated by

Clytemnestra and Aigisthos; according to some versions of the story they married her off to a peasant so that the royal line would end in ignominy. When he grew up, Orestes secretly returned home, accompanied by his friend Pylades. Arriving at the tomb of his father, he laid locks of his hair on the mound, where they were recognised by Elektra, who approached to offer a placatory sacrifice on behalf of her mother; Clytemnestra had had a dream of ill-omen, that she had given birth to a snake which had suckled at her breast and drained away her blood. Orestes quite reasonably saw this as auspicious for himself, and after much agonised discussion of the horrors of matricide, Elektra persuaded Orestes to murder both his mother and Aigisthos. For this terrible deed he was driven insane by the Furies, who pursued him until, at a special trial of the Areopagos at Athens, he was acquitted on the grounds that the murder of a mother is a lesser crime than the murder of a husband. In this way the curse of the house of Atreus was worked out.

Death of Agamemnon *Agamemnon has been trapped in a shroud-like garment in which he is powerless to defend himself. Blood is already spurting from a wound in his chest as he falls backwards against Clytemnestra, while Aigisthos prepares to deliver the final blow. Athenian red-figured calyx-krater (wine-bowl), about 500–480* BC.

The story of Odysseus

Odysseus had known before he ever went to Troy that it would be twenty years before he returned home to his rocky island of Ithaca, his son Telemachos and his wife Penelope. He was at Troy for ten years, and for ten more he travelled across the oceans, shipwrecked, eventually deprived of all his companions, frequently within an inch of his life, until in the twentieth year he landed once more on the shores of his island home.

The Cyclops

On leaving Troy, Odysseus and his companions first encountered the Cicones, whose city they sacked, but at whose hands they suffered heavy losses. They were in danger of losing more of their number to the Lotus Eaters, hedonists who did nothing but sit around and eat the luscious fruit which made them forget all cares and responsibilities. Odysseus had to drag those of his men who had tasted the lotus back to the ships by force, and scarcely had they recovered from this adventure than they landed in the next, their encounter with the Cyclops Polyphemos.

The Cyclopes were a race of huge, one-eyed giants who occupied a fertile country where the soil bore bountiful crops of its own accord and provided rich pasturage for fat sheep and goats with shaggy fleeces. Eager to meet the inhabitants of such a land, Odysseus took one ship into the harbour and, disembarking, walked up with his crew to the cave of the Cyclops Polyphemos, a son of Poseidon. Polyphemos was out tending his sheep, so Odysseus and his crew made themselves at home until he returned with his flocks at dusk. The Cyclops was huge, monstrous and terrible, and after a few perfunctory inquiries into the origins and business of his unexpected guests, he picked up a couple of them and dashed their brains out on the floor before devouring them whole. The Cyclops then fell heavily asleep; Odysseus contemplated stabbing him to death, but gave up the idea when he realised that escape would then be impossible, since the mouth of the cave was blocked with a vast rock, which the Cyclops could lift with one hand, but which the combined strength of Odysseus and his companions was unable to shift. The Cyclops had two more of Odysseus's men for breakfast and then went out, taking care to replace the huge stone at the cave entrance. The resourceful Odysseus was not slow to think up a plan of action. He sharpened a great wooden stake which lay in the cave and hardened its tip in the fire.

Odysseus escaping from the Cyclops' cave *(above left) Odysseus, sword in hand, clings upside-down beneath a large ram, the leader of Polyphemos's flock; he thereby passes safely through the doorway of the cave. Athenian 'Six Technique' lekythos (oil-flask), about 500–480 BC.*

Odysseus and the Cyclops *(above right) The gigantic Cyclops sits holding the wine-cup with which Odysseus has made him drunk; his mouth opens in pain, as Odysseus and his men drive the sharpened stake into his eye. Proto-Attic amphora (wine-jar), about 700 BC.*

When evening came and Polyphemos returned home, Odysseus offered him a bowl of strong wine to wash down his ration of Greek sailors. The Cyclops swallowed the wine with enthusiasm and asked for three refills. Then, in a drunken stupor, he lay down to sleep. Before he nodded off, he asked to know the name of his guest, and Odysseus replied that it was 'Outis', the Greek for 'Nobody'; the Cyclops promised that in return for the wine he would eat 'Nobody' last. As the monster lay asleep, Odysseus heated the tip of the stake in the fire; when it was red-hot he and four of his best men drove the point straight into the Cyclops's one eye. The eye hissed and sizzled, like 'the loud hiss that comes from a great axe or adze when a smith plunges it into cold water to temper it and give strength to the iron'. The Cyclops, rudely awakened by the terrible pain, bellowed and raged, calling out for his neighbours, the other Cyclopes, to come and help. But when they gathered outside his cave and asked who was disturbing him, who had hurt him, he could only reply that Nobody was disturbing him, Nobody was hurting him, upon which they lost interest and went away.

At dawn Odysseus and his men prepared to make their escape from the cave; each man was tied beneath three big woolly sheep, while Odysseus himself clung under the leader of the flock, a huge ram with a magnificent fleece. The blinded Cyclops rolled aside the stone and sat at the door of his cave, trying to catch Odysseus's crew slipping out with the sheep, but they passed safely beneath his hands, Odysseus last of all. Driving the sheep down to their ship, they quickly set sail, although Odysseus was unable to resist taunting the Cyclops, who responded by hurling bits of cliff in the direction of his voice, some coming rather too close to the vessel for comfort. So Odysseus rejoined the rest of the fleet, and while the crews mourned their lost companions, they consoled themselves by feasting on the very sheep that had assisted their escape from the cave.

Aiolia

From the island of the Cyclops, Odysseus sailed on till he reached the floating island of Aiolia, whose king, Aiolos, had been entrusted by Zeus with power over all the winds. Aiolos and his large family received Odysseus and his crew hospitably, and when the time came for them to leave, Aiolos gave Odysseus a leather pouch in which he had imprisoned all the boisterous winds; he then summoned up a gentle westerly breeze which would blow the ships safely home to Ithaca. They sailed on course for ten days and were within sight of Ithaca when disaster overtook them. Odysseus, who had stayed awake to steer the ship for the whole journey, fell into an exhausted sleep, and his crew, who did not know what was in the leather pouch, began to suspect

Aiolos *The male figure may represent Aiolos, King of the Winds, marshalling the dance of the Clouds or Breezes. Athenian red-figured 'knucklebone vase' (of uncertain function), about 460–440 BC.*

that it contained valuable treasure given to Odysseus by Aiolos. They were jealous, feeling that as they had shared Odysseus's hardships, so they should share his rewards: they opened up the bag and accidentally let loose the winds. Odysseus awoke to a raging tempest, which buffeted the ship right back to Aiolia. This time the reception of Odysseus and his comrades was very different. They begged Aiolos to give them another chance, but he, declaring that Odysseus must be a man hated by the gods, declined absolutely to help, and drove him and his shipmates from the door.

Circe

At their next landfall, Laistrygonia, all the ships except Odysseus's own were lost in a calamitous encounter with the monstrous inhabitants, so it was in a state of considerable grief and depression that Odysseus and his surviving comrades found themselves at the island of Aeaea. Disembarking, they lay for two days and nights on the beach, utterly exhausted by their exertions and demoralised by the horrors they had been through. On the third day Odysseus roused himself to explore the island, and from a hilltop he saw smoke rising from a habitation in the woods. Prudently deciding not to reconnoitre at once, he returned to the ship to tell his companions the news. They were predictably dismayed, remembering the Laistrygonians and the Cyclops, but since Odysseus was determined to explore, he divided his company into two groups, one commanded by himself and the other by a man called Eurylochos. The two parties drew lots and the task of exploration fell to Eurylochos, while Odysseus remained at the ship. In due course Eurylochos's party arrived at the house in the woods. Outside were wolves and lions, who gambolled and fawned upon the men; they were in fact human beings who had been given animal shape by the sorceress Circe, whose beautiful singing could be heard inside the house. When the sailors shouted to attract her attention, she came out and invited them to enter; only Eurylochos, suspecting a trick, remained outside. Circe offered the men food, but with it she mixed a drug which caused them to forget their native land; and when they had finished, she struck them with her wand and drove them off into the pig-sties, for they were now to outward appearances swine, though unhappily for them they still remembered who they really were.

The panic-stricken Eurylochos rushed back to the ship to report the disappearance of his companions. Odysseus commanded the man to take him back to Circe's home, and when he refused, set off alone to the rescue. On his way across the island he met Hermes, disguised as a youth; the god gave him a plant called Moly which, mixed with Circe's food, would provide an antidote to her drug; he also instructed him as to how he could get the better of the sorceress: when Circe struck him with her wand, he should rush at her as though to kill her; she would then shrink back in fear and invite him to share her bed. To this he should agree, but he must first extract from her a solemn oath not to try any tricks while he was vulnerable.

Everything happened just as Hermes had predicted. After they had been to bed together, Circe bathed and dressed Odysseus in fine clothes and had a sumptuous banquet prepared for him, but he sat in silent abstraction, refusing all attention. Eventually Circe asked him what was wrong, and he pointed out that she could hardly expect him to be the life and soul of the party while half his crew were languishing outside in the pig-sties. So Circe released the new pigs from their confinement and smeared a magic ointment over them; their bristles fell away, and they became men again, but younger and more handsome than they had ever been before. Odysseus and his men wept for relief and happiness, and only broke off when Circe suggested they should summon the rest of their company to join in the celebrations. They all stayed with Circe for an entire year, eating and drinking and enjoying themselves, forgetting the trials through which they had passed.

The Underworld

Eventually Odysseus was reminded by some of his companions that perhaps it was time to think of Ithaca. Circe warned him that before he could set sail for home he must first visit the Underworld to consult the Theban prophet Teiresias: only Teiresias could give him instructions for his return. So Odysseus sailed across the River of Ocean and moored his ship by Persephone's poplar grove. There on the shore he dug a trench, around which he poured libations to the dead of honey, water, milk and wine; over the trench he cut the throats of a ram and a black sheep. Attracted by the smell of blood, the souls of the dead thronged up to drink, but Odysseus drew his sword and kept them back, waiting for the soul of Teiresias to appear. First to approach was one of his crew, Elpenor, who had fallen off the roof of Circe's house where he had been sleeping on the morning of the departure, and whom in their haste to depart they had left unburied and unwept; this state of affairs

Circe *Circe stands in the centre, stirring the cup she has just taken from one of Odysseus's men, who now has the head of a boar. Four of his companions are shown, with the heads of a boar, ram, lion and wolf. On the far left Odysseus is approaching with drawn sword. Athenian black-figured 'Merrythought' cup, about 550–530 BC.*

Odysseus promised to rectify as soon as he could. When Teiresias appeared, Odysseus let him drink the blood, and the prophet then told him that he had a good chance of returning home safely, but that he must be sure not to plunder the Cattle of the Sun on the island of Thrinakie; he also warned him of the situation he would find on Ithaca, where rapacious suitors were wooing his faithful wife Penelope.

After he had heard all that Teiresias could tell him, Odysseus let other ghosts approach and drink the blood which enabled them to converse with him. The first to come was his ancient mother, who relayed to him the manner of her death, and a sad account of the wretched state of his father Laertes and of Penelope's brave efforts to fend off her suitors. Odysseus, overcome by grief and desiring to comfort both himself and his mother, tried three times to embrace her, but three times she slipped wraith-like through his hands and left him holding the air. Other heroines approached and conversed, and after them came Agamemnon, who told Odysseus of his bloody death, comforting him with the thought that Penelope would never act as Clytemnestra had done. Achilles also approached, and Odysseus hailed him as the most fortunate man who ever lived, a mighty prince among the living and the dead. Achilles replied that he would rather be a slave and alive than king among the dead, but Odysseus was able to cheer him up with news of the prowess of his son Neoptolemos, and he departed happy.

During his visit Odysseus saw some of the famous sights of the Underworld: Sisyphus endlessly pushing his great boulder up a mountain, with it always slipping back just as it reached the top; and Tantalus, standing up to his neck in a pool of water which vanished as he bent to drink, with branches of fruits dangling above his head that blew away as he reached to grasp them. Odysseus was keen to see more, and he did meet the ghost of the mighty Herakles, but before he could encounter other heroes of earlier generations he was overwhelmed by a great wave of the dead who came up in their thousands and raised around him their mournful, haunting cry; panic-stricken, he returned to his ship, loosened the moorings and crossed back to the world of the living.

The Sirens and Skylla and Charybdis

Odysseus returned to Circe's island and, once Elpenor was properly buried, Circe was able to give Odysseus further instructions for his journey and to prepare him for some of the evils to come. The ship sailed first by the island of the Sirens, terrible creatures with the heads and voices of women and the bodies of birds, who existed for the purpose of luring mariners on to the rocks of their island with their sweet songs. As the ship approached, a dead calm fell upon the sea, and the crew took to their oars. On Circe's instructions Odysseus plugged the ears of the crew with wax while he had himself bound to the mast, so that they would carry him safely past the danger yet let him listen to the song. 'Draw near, Odysseus,' sang the Sirens:

Skylla *With her left arm Skylla reaches over to pull one of Odysseus's men out of the ship; the dogs at her waist are mauling two others, while a fourth is caught in the grip of a powerful fish-tail. Roman bronze bowl, first century* AD.

> No seaman ever sailed his black ship past this spot without listening to the sweet tones that flow from our lips ... we know all that the Argives and Trojans suffered on the broad plain of Troy by the will of the gods, and we have foreknowledge of all that is going to happen on this fruitful earth ...

Odysseus shouted to his men to release him, but they rowed resolutely on, and eventually the danger was passed.

Their next task was to navigate the twin hazards of Skylla and Charybdis. Charybdis was a terrifying whirlpool, alternately sucking down and throwing up the heaving water; the cautious mariner who chose to avoid her was forced instead to encounter the equally horrific Skylla. Skylla lurked in a cavern set high up in a rock, concealed by spray and mist from the breakers below; she had twelve feet which dangled in the air and six necks, each equipped with a monstrous head with triple rows of teeth. From her cavern she exacted a toll of human victims from the ships which passed beneath. Odysseus, forewarned by Circe, chose not to tell his sailors about Skylla; giving Charybdis as wide a berth as possible, they passed directly under Skylla's rock, and although Odysseus was armed and prepared to do battle with her for the lives of his crew, she managed to evade his watch and succeeded in snatching up six shrieking victims.

The Cattle of the Sun

Next the ship came within sight of the island of Thrinakie, a place of rich pasturage where Apollo kept his herds of fat cattle. Odysseus had been warned by both Circe and Teiresias that if he hoped to reach Ithaca alive he should avoid this place and must not at any cost lay a hand upon the cattle. He explained this to his men, but they, weary and depressed by the loss of six more comrades, insisted on making anchor and spending the night on the beach. Faced with a mutiny, Odysseus had little option but to comply, but he made them swear to leave the cattle strictly alone. That night a storm set in, and for a full month the wind blew from the south, making it impossible for them to continue their journey.

So long as they still had the provisions Circe had given them, the men kept to their oath and did not touch the cattle. But eventually their food ran out and, driven by hunger, they seized the opportunity presented by Odysseus's temporary absence from the ship to round up some of the best of the herd; they reasoned that if they slaughtered them in honour of the gods, the gods could hardly be angry. Odysseus returned to the smell of roasting meat; rebuke was useless for the deed was done, and the gods were determined to avenge the crime. When the meat was finished, the wind dropped, so the ship could set sail; but no sooner was she fairly out to sea than a terrible gale sprung up and the ship was first smashed by the force of the waves, then rent asunder by a lightning flash. All hands were lost save Odysseus himself, who managed to cling on to the wreckage of the mast and keel, which he rode for ten days until he was washed up on the shores of the island of Ogygia, home of the beautiful nymph Calypso.

Calypso

Calypso made Odysseus her lover and he stayed with her for seven years as he had no means of escape. Eventually the goddess Athena sent Hermes, messenger of the gods, to explain to the nymph that the time had come for her to send her visitor on his way. Calypso, though reluctant to lose him, knew she must obey, so she provided Odysseus with the materials for a raft, gave him food and drink, and summoned up a favourable wind to speed him towards Ithaca. Without incident, he came within sight of the land of the Phaiacians, great seafarers who were destined to carry him on the last lap of his journey. But then Poseidon intervened; he hated Odysseus for what he had done to his son, the Cyclops Polyphemos, and now he was outraged to see him so near to the end of his journey. So he sent up yet another storm, which broke the mast off the raft and left it to be flung around by the winds.

As the north wind at harvest-time tosses about the fields a ball of thistles that have stuck together, so did the gusts drive his craft hither and thither over the sea. Now the South Wind would toss it to the North to play with, and now the East would leave it for the West to chase.

Odysseus was saved from certain death by the intervention of the sea-nymph Ino. She gave him her veil, instructing him to wrap it round his waist and then abandon ship and strike out for the shore. As a huge wave snapped his raft into matchwood, Odysseus did as he was told. For two days and nights he swam onwards, but on the third day he reached the shores of Phaiacia and eventually managed to land on the rocky coast at the mouth of a river. He threw Ino's veil back into the water and lay down in a thicket to sleep.

Odysseus in Phaiacia

Inspired by Athena, the Phaiacian princess Nausikaa had chosen that very day to make an expedition to the mouth of the river to wash clothes in the deep pools there. When she and her maids had finished the washing and spread it out on the shingle, they bathed, ate and then amused themselves singing and playing with a ball as they waited for the clothes to dry. As Nausikaa threw the ball to one of the maids, the maid missed and the ball fell in the river; all the girls shrieked loudly and Odysseus awoke from sleep, wondering what savage land he had arrived at now. Breaking off a branch with which to conceal his nakedness, he emerged from his thicket to find Nausikaa standing her ground bravely while the other girls fled in panic. He addressed Nausikaa as a suppliant, begging her to show him the way to the city and give him some rag to wear. Nausikaa answered him with dignity and kindness, and after he had washed, anointed himself with oil and dressed himself in some of their fine clean clothing, she gave him food and drink, and then he accompanied the girls back to the outskirts of the city. To avoid gossip Nausikaa left Odysseus there to finish the journey into the centre alone. She suggested he should make straight for the house of her father Alkinous, and fall as a suppliant at the knees of her mother Arete.

Guided by Athena herself in the guise of another local girl, Odysseus arrived at Alkinous's splendid palace. There were walls of bronze and gates of gold, guarded by gold and silver watchdogs. Inside the hall, light was provided by solid gold statues of youths holding torches. Outside the courtyard was a beautiful garden and orchard, with fruit trees, vines and a well-watered vegetable patch. After he had admired all this, Odysseus, wrapped in a cloud of mist provided by Athena, passed inside and walked straight up to Queen Arete, around whose knees he flung his arms in supplication. As the concealing mist rolled away, the Phaiacians listened in amazement to his petition: he asked for shelter and to be conveyed home to his native land.

When he had overcome his initial astonishment, Alkinous was generous in his reaction. Politely forbearing to question his guest at once, he arranged for his immediate refreshment, promising that in the morning steps would be taken to restore him to his homeland. When the other Phaiacians went home and Odysseus was alone with Alkinous and his wife, Arete asked him who he was and how he had acquired his clothes, which she had not been slow to recognise. So Odysseus told them the story of his adventures since leaving the island of Ogygia, explaining how he had met Nausikaa at the river mouth. Meanwhile Arete arranged for a bed to be made up, and Odysseus was grateful to retire.

The next day a ship was made ready to convey Odysseus home, but before he could set out, the hospitable Alkinous insisted on feasting his guest and regaling him with sports and other entertainment. First the bard Demodokos performed for the assembled company, singing of an episode in the Trojan War, a quarrel which had taken place between the illustrious Achilles and the cunning Odysseus. As he listened, Odysseus wept and drew his mantle over his head to conceal his misery. Only Alkinous noticed, and to cheer his guest up he proposed some athletic contests. Odysseus was at first content to watch the young noblemen, but when taunted he threw the discus a record-breaking length. Dancing followed, and then Demodokos sang again, the story of the amorous adventures of Aphrodite and Ares. The Phaiacian noblemen now vied with one another to shower presents on Odysseus. At the evening meal Demodokos sang again, and at Odysseus's suggestion his theme was the Wooden Horse of Troy. Odysseus wept again as he listened, and again Alkinous alone observed him. At the end of the story, Alkinous asked Odysseus to tell them who he was, where he came from and where he wished to be conveyed; and why he wept at Demodokos's songs. Thus invited, Odysseus told them who he was and described all the adventures he had been through: he spoke of the Cicones and the Lotus Eaters, of the Cyclops, Aiolos, the Laistrygonians, Circe, his visit to the Underworld, the Sirens, Skylla and Charybdis and the Cattle of the Sun, ending with his stay with Calypso, the escape from whose island had brought him to the land of the Phaiacians.

The following evening Odysseus at last said goodbye to his hosts and a swift Phaiacian ship bore him smoothly over the sea to Ithaca. Odysseus slept as the ship surged forward, and was still asleep when the morning star arose and the crew deposited him along with the gifts the Phaiacians had given him on the shores of Ithaca, beside a beautiful cave, home of the nymphs. When Odysseus awoke he failed to recognise the spot, largely because Athena had cast a mist over the island, to give herself time to meet Odysseus and arrange a suitable disguise for him. As he was dismally wondering where the treacherous Phaiacians had landed him, Athena appeared to him in the guise of a shepherd and, in response to his enquiries, told him that he was indeed in Ithaca. The wary Odysseus spun the goddess a story about being a Cretan exile; she smiled at his cunning, and in reply revealed her true identity, reassured him that he really was in Ithaca, and counselled him on how he should proceed in order to regain his wife and kingdom.

Odysseus in Ithaca

In the twenty years that Odysseus had been absent from home most people on Ithaca, apart from his wife Penelope, his son Telemachos and a few faithful retainers, had come to believe that he was dead, that he had perished either at Troy or on the voyage home. Since Penelope was not only beautiful and accomplished but also rich and powerful, and the man who married her would succeed to Odysseus's wealth and status, she was besieged by suitors, young noblemen who lounged around in her husband's palace, eating and drinking his provisions and forcing their unwelcome attentions upon her. For as long as she could Penelope played for time, persuading each that he had grounds for hope but saying nothing definite to any of them. For three years she tricked them into waiting, by announcing that she was weaving a winding-shroud for Odysseus's old father Laertes; it would be unseemly were he to die with no shroud ready for him, and they must wait for her decision until she had finished her work. Every day she worked away at the loom, but when night fell she undid her work by torch-light. As the fourth year began, however,

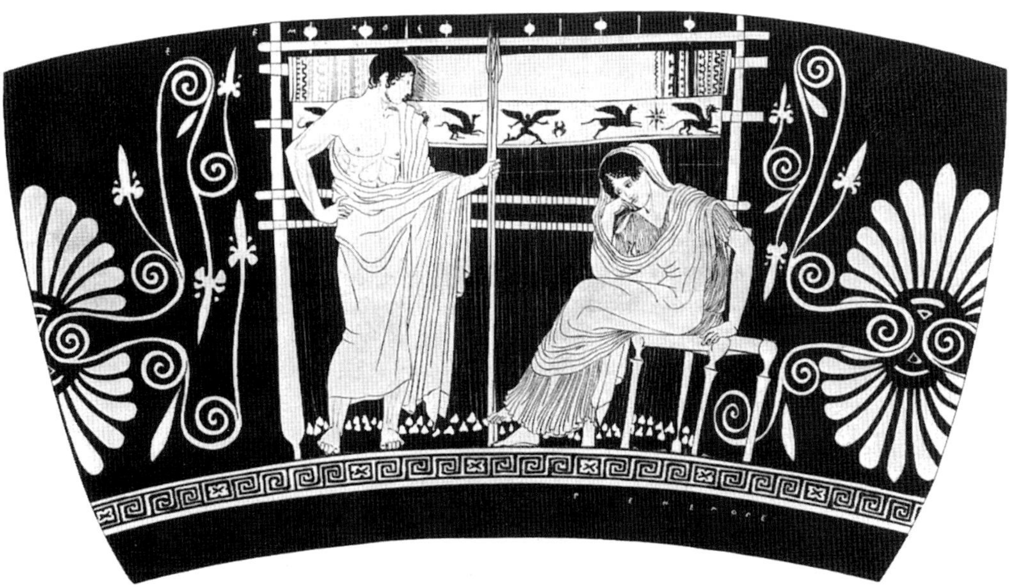

Penelope at her loom *One of her suitors confronts Penelope in front of her loom. Her dejected attitude suggests that her trick of weaving by day and undoing the work by night has been discovered. Athenian red-figured skyphos (drinking-cup), about 460–440 BC.*

she was betrayed by one of her maids, who helped the suitors catch her at her scheme, and reluctantly she was forced to finish her web.

Shortly before Odysseus's arrival in Ithaca, Athena had inspired Telemachos, now of an age to play an active part in his father's return, to set out on a journey with the aim of discovering what had happened to him. Telemachos travelled first to Pylos, where he consulted the ancient Nestor; Nestor had no news, but sent him on to the magnificent palace of Menelaos at Sparta. Menelaos and Helen treated him with great kindness, and Menelaos explained how he had heard from the Old Man of the Sea that Odysseus was marooned on the island of the beautiful nymph Calypso. When Odysseus himself landed on Ithaca, Telemachos was on his way home; the suitors, irritated and somewhat alarmed by Telemachos's grown-up behaviour, were planning to ambush his ship on its return journey, but with the aid of Athena Telemachos successfully evaded their trap and arrived safely in Ithaca.

Athena had advised Odysseus not to go straight into the town but instead to seek shelter with the swineherd Eumaios, who lived with his pigs on a farm some distance outside. Disguised as a tramp, Odysseus did as his patroness suggested, and was very kindly received by Eumaios, whose explanation of the situation in the town was interspersed with much praise of his absent master and prayers for his safe return. In response to Eumaios's questions, Odysseus told him a long story about his origins, saying he was the illegitimate son of a wealthy Cretan; after numerous adventures he had ended up in Thesprotia, where he heard of Odysseus, who had lately passed that way. The king of Thesprotia put him on a ship bound for Dulichium, but the rascally crew had stripped and bound him, intending to sell him as a slave. When they disembarked on Ithaca, he had managed to slip his ropes and swim ashore, so arriving at the homestead of Eumaios.

Eumaios swallowed all of this story except the reference to Odysseus, which he refused to accept, even when his guest swore that Odysseus would be home that very month and offered to let Eumaios's men throw him from a precipice if he were proved wrong. Eumaios served Odysseus a meal of roast pork and spread him a comfortable bed by the fire; he himself spent the night outside, watching over his absent master's property.

The next evening, over supper in the swineherd's hut, Odysseus announced his intention of travelling into the town to beg at the palace; but Eumaios, anxious for the safety of his guest, insisted that he await the return of Telemachos. That evening it was Eumaios's turn to recount his life story, and he told how he had been born of noble parentage but kidnapped by some Phoenician traders when a child, to be sold into slavery on Ithaca. Early the next morning Telemachos landed on the island and, guided by Athena, went straight to the swineherd's hut. While Eumaios walked to the town to tell Penelope that Telemachos was back, Athena dissolved Odysseus's disguise and prompted him to reveal his identity to his son. Telemachos was at first reluctant to accept that the beggar by the swineherd's hearth was really his father, but eventually he was convinced and the two wept together for joy and relief. Recovering, they laid their plans: Odysseus would follow Telemachos back to the town and go to beg in his own palace. There he would assess the situation and wait for the right time to attack; when that time arrived he would signal to Telemachos and the two of them, with the help of Zeus and Athena, would set about the destruction of the miserable suitors.

Odysseus travelled to the town in the company of the swineherd. On the way they met the goatherd Melantheus, a scoundrel completely in the pay of the suitors, who levelled a number of insults and blows at the old beggar. Outside the palace on a dung heap lay an ancient hound, mangy and diseased. When he heard Odysseus's voice he lowered his ears and feebly wagged his tail. Odysseus recognised him at once and, much affected by his appearance, quietly brushed aside a tear. As he commented on the dog's dilapidated appearance to Eumaios, the latter replied that twenty years ago no dog could have outrun Argos or picked up a scent faster, but in his master's absence he had grown old and neglected. As the two passed into the building, Argos quietly expired, happy to have seen his master again after twenty long years.

Predictably, Odysseus was abused and insulted by the suitors when he tried to beg from them in his own hall. They jeered at his rags, threatened him, and one even threw a stool at him. But once he had defeated the resident beggar in a wrestling match, they thought more highly of him. At this point Penelope was suddenly inspired to show herself to her suitors. So she descended to the hall, where her beauty filled them all with desire; she chided Telemachos for allowing them to insult a beggar in her house, and then she turned to the suitors and suggested that instead of eating her out of house and home it would be more seemly for them to bring her presents. They agreed and, much to Odysseus's delight, produced fine gifts of cloth and jewellery. As the evening drew on, it became time for another banquet and Odysseus made himself useful tending the lights and the fires. The suitors again taunted the beggar in their midst, and another stool was thrown, only to be adroitly avoided by its target. When the suitors finally withdrew to their own homes for the night, Telemachos and Odysseus removed all the weapons from the hall and put them away in a storeroom. Penelope then came down again to speak to the beggar, whose presence had aroused her interest. She asked him where he had come from and explained her own miserable situation: the suitors were pressing her to choose between them, while she longed only for the return of Odysseus. He told her he was a Cretan of royal descent, and that he had met Odysseus in Crete. To test the truth of his story she asked him what clothes Odysseus had been wearing, and he described a purple cloak and a gold brooch with a device of a hound gripping a fawn. Penelope wept when she recognised these details. To cheer her up, Odysseus promised her that her husband was alive and well and very close; in fact, he would be back in Ithaca that very month.

Penelope now suggested that the beggar would enjoy a bath and a com-

Odysseus and Eurykleia *As Eurykleia washes the beggar's feet, she feels the scar on his leg and recognises him as Odysseus. Athenian red-figured skyphos (drinking-cup), about 460–440 BC.*

fortable bed. The cautious Odysseus, however, would only allow his feet to be washed by an elderly maid, and so the old nurse Eurykleia was summoned for the task. Eurykleia immediately commented on how the beggar reminded her of Odysseus; Odysseus replied that everyone said so. As she started to wash his feet, Odysseus suddenly remembered the scar on his leg, acquired when he was just a boy and had joined an expedition to hunt wild boar on Mount Parnassus with his grandfather Autolykos and his uncles. He turned into the shadows, but sure enough Eurykleia felt and recognised the scar; in her excitement she dropped the bowl of water and would have shouted aloud to alert Penelope had not Odysseus grasped her firmly by the throat and instructed her not to tell a soul who he was until he had got rid of the suitors. All this time Penelope had been sitting absorbed in her own thoughts. But when Eurykleia had fetched more water and finished her task and Odysseus was once more seated by the fire, she turned to him again, and again explained her quandary: should she marry and so rid Telemachos of the burden of her presence and that of the suitors, or continue to hold out for Odysseus's return? She asked if the beggar could tell her the meaning of a recent dream in which a great eagle had swooped down from the hills and fallen upon her twenty pet geese, killing them all; then, perching on a roofbeam, the bird had told her that the geese were the suitors and he himself was Odysseus.

The beggar Odysseus assured her that the dream would come true and that the suitors were all doomed, but the cautious Penelope replied that dreams were confusing things; those which issued through the gate of horn came true, but those from the gate of ivory came only to deceive. Before she retired to her quarters for the night, to weep for Odysseus until she slept, she told the beggar that she intended to announce a competition for the suitors. She would set up twelve axe-heads in a line and invite the suitors to string the great bow of Odysseus and shoot an arrow straight through all the twelve. She would marry whoever proved himself able to accomplish this feat, which Odysseus himself had frequently performed.

The next day Penelope brought out the great bow of Odysseus and announced the competition to the suitors, each of whom hoped that he would be the only one to string the bow and shoot through the axe-heads. Telemachos prepared the hall for the contest and then tried to string the huge bow himself, bending it across his knee. It required all his strength, yet he would have managed it had he not been stopped by a nod from Odysseus. So he abandoned the attempt and one by one the suitors took their turn, but none could string the bow, let alone shoot an arrow straight through the axe-heads. While they were trying their strength, Odysseus slipped out of the hall and revealed his true identity to the swineherd Eumaios and the equally trustworthy oxherd, Philoetius, instructing them to come to his assistance when he gave them the sign. When one of the two leaders of the suitors, Eurymachos, had tried and failed the test, the other leader, Antinous, suggested they should put it aside for the day, since it was a feast day and they should be banqueting and sacrificing to the archer-god Apollo: his suggestion met with general approval. After they had all drunk their first toast, Odysseus asked if he might be allowed to try the bow. Antinous objected, but Penelope, who had been watching, insisted he should be allowed to have a go; Telemachos then intervened, sending his mother back to her chamber. In the general hubbub the swineherd Eumaios quietly took the bow up to Odysseus and placed it in his hands. He turned the familiar weapon this way and that, checking that it was whole and undamaged by its long rest; then, 'as easily as a musician who knows his lyre strings the cord on a new peg after looping the twisted sheep-gut at both ends', he strung the bow and twanged the cord, which sang under his hands like the call of a swallow. Quietly, without fuss, he fitted an arrow to the string and shot through the entire line of axes.

The suitors, dumbfounded, were still more shocked by the sequel. For as Telemachos stepped up to take his place beside his father, Odysseus aimed a second arrow, this time at the throat of Antinous. Not realising what was happening and thinking it had been an accident, the suitors rounded on Odysseus in a fury, but when he told them who he was and that his intention was to slay the lot of them, they became properly aware of their predicament and turned to attack him. Backed up by the faithful swineherd and oxherd, Odysseus and Telemachos might still have been overpowered by the sheer numbers of the suitors had not Athena herself intervened on their side. As suitor after suitor fell to the floor, only the minstrel and the herald, pressed into the suitors' service against their will, were spared. The suitors 'lay in heaps in the blood and dust, like fish that the fishermen have dragged out of the grey surf in the meshes of their net on to a bend of the beach, to lie in masses on the sand gasping for the salt sea water till the bright sun ends their lives'. Then Odysseus, 'spattered with blood and filth, like a lion when he comes from feeding on some farmer's bullock', summoned the aged nurse Eurykleia. She set those maidservants who had disgraced themselves through consorting with the suitors to clean and tidy up the hall; that done, they were hanged in a row in the yard.

Penelope, under Athena's influence, had slept soundly through the noise of the great battle in the hall and the subsequent cleaning-up operations. Now she was aroused by Eurykleia and told the news of her husband's return. Numbed by shock, she could not be entirely sure that the stranger really was Odysseus, or what she should say to him. Cautious as her husband himself, she put him to one final test by instructing Eurykleia to move out of their bedroom the big bed that Odysseus had built. Odysseus knew that the bed was impossible to move, for it was built around a living olive tree. Only when, exasperated by her obstinacy, he had described the construction of the bed was Penelope convinced that he was indeed her long-lost husband; then she threw herself into his arms and wept. So they went together to their marriage bed and lay at last in each other's arms again; Odysseus told Penelope all his adventures, and the night went on and on, as the goddess Athena kept the dawn lingering by the shores of Ocean.

Jason, Medea and the Golden Fleece

The Golden Fleece had originally belonged to the ram which had saved the children of Athamas, Phrixos and Helle from being sacrificed to Zeus at the command of their wicked stepmother Ino. According to the legend, the ram collected the children from their home in Orchomenos and then flew east with them clinging to its back. As they crossed the narrow channel which divides Europe from Asia, Helle fell from the ram's back, giving her name to the sea below, the Hellespont. But Phrixos flew on over the Black Sea until the ram set him down in Kolchis, at the court of King Aeetes. Aeetes received Phrixos kindly, and when the boy had sacrificed the ram to Zeus, he gave its miraculous fleece to the king. Aeetes dedicated the fleece to Ares and hung it in a grove sacred to the war-god, where it was guarded by a fearsome serpent.

Why did Jason want the Golden Fleece? It was not that he coveted it for himself; like other heroes he was required to attempt what was thought to be an impossible deed to satisfy the demands of a hard-hearted taskmaster, in this case Pelias, king of Iolkos. Jason was the son of Aison, the rightful king of Iolkos; Pelias was Aison's half-brother, and in some versions of the story Pelias was supposed to rule only until Jason was old enough to take over. In these circumstances it was hardly surprising that when Jason grew up and demanded his rightful inheritance, Pelias sent him off to bring back the Golden Fleece. The quest for the Fleece is the story of the voyage of the *Argo* and the adventures of her crew, the Argonauts. The legend is probably older than the *Iliad* and the *Odyssey*, but it comes down to us chiefly through a much later epic poem, the *Argonautica* of the Alexandrian poet Apollonios of Rhodes.

There were about fifty Argonauts, and although the sources differ on some of their names, the main characters are clear. Apart from Jason himself, there was Argos, builder of the *Argo*; Tiphys the helmsman; the musician Orpheus; Zetes and Kalais, sons of the North Wind; Helen's brothers, Kastor and Polydeukes; Peleus, father of Achilles; Meleager of Calydonian boar-hunt fame; Laertes and Autolykos, father and grandfather of Odysseus; Admetus, who was later to let his wife die in his place; the prophet Amphiaraos and, for the first part of the journey, Herakles himself; besides these famous names there were a host of other heroes. Their ship, the *Argo*, whose name means

The building of the Argo *One of the Argonauts is working on the vessel's prow, while another adjusts the sail on the yard-arm, assisted by the goddess Athena. Roman terracotta relief ('Campana plaque'), first century* BC *or* AD.

'swift', was the fastest ever built. She was constructed in the port of Pagasai in Thessaly and was made entirely of timber from Mount Pelion, except for the prow, which was a piece of a sacred oak tree brought by the goddess Athena from the sanctuary of Zeus at Dodona. This piece of oak was prophetic, and could on occasion give tongue.

The *Argo* set sail with favourable omens and travelled north towards the Black Sea. On the journey to Kolchis her crew met with numerous adventures. In Mysia they lost Herakles, when another member of the crew, a beautiful youth named Hylas, went off in search of fresh water for a feast and failed to return to the ship. The nymphs of the spring that he found, falling in love with his beauty, had abducted and drowned him; but Herakles refused to give up searching, and so the *Argo* had to sail without him.

On the Greek shore of the Bosporos the Argonauts found Phineus, a blind seer and son of Poseidon, on whom the gods had inflicted a terrible curse. Whenever he sat down to eat, he was visited by a plague of Harpies, terrible creatures part-woman and part-bird, who seized some of the food in their beaks and talons and defiled the rest with their excrement. The Argonauts set a trap for these monsters. They invited Phineus to share their table, and when the Harpies duly appeared, the winged sons of the North Wind drew their swords and pursued them until, exhausted, they promised to desist. Phineus then revealed to them as much as he was able concerning their journey: chief among the hazards they would face were the clashing rocks; when they reached these they should send a dove through first. If the dove found the passage between the rocks, so too would the *Argo*, but if the dove failed, they should turn the ship around, for their mission was doomed to failure.

The dove they sent out did pass safely through the clashing rocks, leaving only its longest tail feather in their grip; *Argo* too sped through the narrow channel, suffering only slight damage to her stern timbers, and without any more significant adventures the Argonauts arrived safely at Kolchis.

When Jason explained why he had come, King Aeetes stipulated that before Jason could remove the Golden Fleece he must first yoke two bronze-footed, fire-breathing bulls, a gift of the god Hephaistos, to a plough; he must then sow some of the teeth of the dragon Kadmos had slain in Thebes (Athena had given these teeth to Aeetes), and when armed men sprang up he must destroy them. Jason rather rashly agreed to all these conditions, but was fortunate enough to receive the help of the king's sorceress daughter Medea in carrying them out. Medea, who first made Jason promise that he would take her back to Iolkos as his wife, gave him a magic ointment to rub over his body and his shield; this made him impervious to all attack, whether of fire or iron. She further instructed him on what to do with the crop of armed men: he should throw stones into their midst so that they would attack each other rather than Jason himself. Thus armed and warned, Jason succeeded in all his tasks.

Aeetes, somewhat surprised at his visitor's prowess, was still reluctant to hand over the Fleece, and even attempted to set fire to the *Argo* and kill her crew. So while Medea drugged the guardian serpent, Jason quickly removed the Golden Fleece from the sacred grove, and with the rest of the Argonauts they slipped quietly away to sea. When Aeetes found both his Fleece and his daughter missing, he gave chase in another ship, but even this had been foreseen by Medea. She had brought along her young brother Apsyrtos, and she now proceeded to murder him and cut him up into small pieces which she threw over the side of the ship. As she had anticipated, Aeetes stopped to pick up the pieces, and so the *Argo* made good her escape.

The route of the homeward journey of the *Argo* has baffled many scholars. Instead of returning through the Hellespont, Jason left the Black Sea via the Danube, which miraculously allowed him to emerge into the Adriatic; not content with this achievement, the *Argo* went on to sail up both the Po and the Rhine before somehow finding her way back into the more familiar waters of the Mediterranean. And everywhere they went the Argonauts met with fantastic adventures. On Crete, for example, they encountered the bronze giant Talos, a creature designed by Hephaistos to operate as a sort of mechanical coastal defence system for Minos, king of Crete. Talos would walk around Crete three times each day, keeping ships away by breaking off portions of the cliffs and hurling them at any vessel that tried to come too close. He was completely invulnerable except for a vein in his foot; if this were damaged, his life-force would leak away. Medea was able to drug him so that he became insane and threw himself about on the rocks, eventually damaging his vein and so bringing about his death.

Medea and the ram *Medea demonstrates her magic recipe for rejuvenation by boiling up a ram; surprisingly, the elderly man watching the experiment is not Pelias but Jason himself. Athenian red-figured hydria (water-jar), about 480 BC.*

When Jason finally arrived back in Iolkos, he married Medea and gave the Golden Fleece to Pelias. There are various accounts of what happened next. One version of the story is that Medea tricked the daughters of Pelias into murdering their father. She first demonstrated her powers of rejuvenation by mixing various potions in a cauldron of boiling water, then slaughtering and chopping up an aged ram and dropping in the pieces: immediately a fresh young lamb emerged. Fired with enthusiasm and with the best of intentions, Pelias's daughters hurried to cut up their old father and boil his pieces in the cauldron; unfortunately they succeeded only in hastening his end.

In the ensuing scandal Jason and Medea fled to Corinth, where they lived happily for at least ten years and had two children of their own. Eventually, however, Jason grew tired of his wife and tried to leave her for Glauke, the young daughter of the king of Corinth. Medea, furious with jealousy, sent Glauke a gift of a robe which, when she put it on, clung to her skin and tore it off; as her father tried to help his tortured daughter he too became entangled and they both perished miserably. To punish Jason still further, Medea went on to murder their own children, before escaping into the sky in a fiery chariot. Jason eventually returned to rule in Iolkos.

Perseus and Medusa

According to the Alexandrian scholar Apollodoros, Perseus, the legendary founder of Mycenae, would never have been born at all if his grandfather had had his way. Akrisios, king of Argos, was the father of a beautiful daughter, Danae, but he was disappointed to have no son. When he consulted an oracle about his lack of a male heir, he was told that he would produce no son himself, but that in the course of time he would have a grandson, whose destiny it was to kill his grandfather. Akrisios took strenuous steps to evade his fate. He shut Danae up in a tower of bronze, and there she languished in total seclusion until the day when she was visited by Zeus in the form of a shower of gold; subsequently she gave birth to Perseus. Akrisios was furious, but still thought his destiny could be avoided. He made his carpenter construct a large chest into which Danae was forced to climb along with her baby and they were then pushed out to sea. However, they survived the waves, and after a tiresome journey the chest was washed up on the shores of Seriphos, one of the islands of the Cyclades. Here Danae and Perseus were found and looked after by an honest fisherman, Dictys, brother of the less scrupulous king of Seriphos, Polydektes.

In time Polydektes fell in love with Danae, but as he grew up Perseus protected his mother jealously from the king's unwelcome advances. One day at a banquet Polydektes asked his guests what gift each was prepared to offer him. The others all promised horses, but Perseus volunteered to fetch him the gorgon's head. When Polydektes took him at his word, Perseus was forced to make his offer good. There were three gorgons, monstrous winged creatures with snaky hair; two were immortal but the third, Medusa, was mortal and so potentially vulnerable; the difficulty was that anyone who looked at her was turned to stone. Fortunately, Hermes came to the rescue, and showed Perseus the way to the Graiai, three ancient sisters who shared one eye and one tooth between them. Instructed by Hermes, Perseus managed to get hold of the eye and the tooth and refused to return them until the Graiai showed him the way to the Nymphs who would provide him with the equipment he needed to deal with Medusa. The Nymphs obligingly provided a cap of darkness which would enable Perseus to take Medusa by surprise, winged boots to help him make his escape and a special bag to put the head in once he had sawn it off. Hermes produced a sickle-shaped knife, and so Perseus set off fully equipped to find Medusa. With the help of Athena, who held up a bronze mirror in which he could see the gorgon's reflection

Danae, Perseus and Akrisios *Akrisios directs his carpenter to put the final touches to the chest in which he proposes to push Danae and Perseus out to sea. Danae and the nurse holding the child remonstrate with Akrisios, but Perseus himself seems more interested in the carpenter's actions. Athenian red-figured hydria (water-jar), about 490 BC.*

Perseus and the gorgon *Perseus stabs the gorgon Medusa in the throat. He looks away, because any mortal who saw her face would turn to stone. The god Hermes stands watching on the right. Athenian black-figured oinochoe (wine-jug), about 540 BC.*

Andromeda *The Ethiopian princess, supported by two slaves, watches the preparation of the stakes to which she will be tied to await the arrival of the sea-monster. Her father sits beyond the stakes, his head in his hands; off the picture to the right is Perseus, coming to the rescue. Athenian red-figured hydria (water-jar), about 450* BC.

rather than looking on her terrible face, he finally managed to despatch her. Packing the head safely into his satchel, he sped off back towards Seriphos, assisted by his winged boots.

As he flew over the coast of Ethiopia, Perseus saw below him a beautiful princess tied to a rock. This was Andromeda, whose foolish mother Cassiopia had incurred the wrath of Poseidon by boasting that she was more beautiful than the daughters of the sea-god Nereus. To punish her Poseidon sent a sea-monster to ravage the kingdom; it would be appeased only if offered the king's daughter, Andromeda, who was duly placed on the shore to wait a terrible fate. Perseus fell in love at once, killed the sea-monster and freed the princess. Her joyful parents offered him Andromeda as a wife, and the two left together to continue the journey to Seriphos. Polydektes had not believed Perseus would ever return, and so it must have been rather gratifying for Perseus to watch the tyrant slowly petrify under the gaze of the gorgon's head. Perseus then gave the head to Athena, who fixed it as an emblem in the centre of her breast-plate.

Perseus, Danae and Andromeda now set off together for Argos, where they hoped to be reconciled with the old king Akrisios. But when Akrisios heard they were coming, he fled from the threat of his grandson's presence into Thessaly where, unknown to each other, both Perseus and Akrisios found themselves at the funeral games of the king of Larissa. Here the oracle that Akrisios had feared came true, for as Perseus threw a discus, it swerved off course and fell upon Akrisios's foot as he stood among the onlookers, killing him outright.

Perseus sensibly decided it would not be a very popular move to return home to Argos and claim Akrisios's throne when he had just killed him, so instead he exchanged kingdoms with his cousin Megapenthes. Megapenthes went to Argos while Perseus ruled in Tiryns, where he is said to have been responsible for the fortifications of Midea and Mycenae.

Oedipus and the Theban Cycle

The cycle of myths concerned with the fortunes of the city of Thebes and its royal family is certainly as old as the stories which make up the *Iliad* and the *Odyssey*, but it comes to us largely through much later sources. While the foundation of Thebes is chiefly known from Roman authors such as the poet Ovid, the stories of Pentheus and Oedipus are told by the tragedians of fifth-century Athens, Aeschylus, Sophocles and Euripides.

Kadmos and the foundation of Thebes

Kadmos was one of three sons of Agenor, king of Tyre on the eastern shore of the Mediterranean. Their sister, the beautiful Europa, was playing on the seashore when she was carried off across the sea to Crete by Zeus in the form of a bull. Agenor told his sons to find their sister and not to return home without her. In the course of his wanderings Kadmos arrived at Delphi, where the oracle advised him that a cow would meet him as he left the sanctuary; he was instructed to found a city at the place where the cow finally lay down. The animal led him to the site of the future Thebes. When she lay down to rest, Kadmos recognised that this was the place for his city and he decided to sacrifice the cow to the gods. Needing fresh water, he sent his attendants to fetch it from a nearby spring, the fountain of Ares. The fountain pool, however, was guarded by a dreadful serpent, which attacked and devoured all Kadmos's men. When Kadmos came in search of them, he found only fragments of limbs and the huge monster lying sated. Single-handed and lightly armed as he was, he managed to slay the snake, and then, on the advice of Athena, he sowed its teeth in the ground. Up sprang a crop of warriors, fully armed with swords and spears. They would have turned on Kadmos, had he not had the idea of throwing a great boulder in their midst; at this they began to hack each other to pieces, continuing until only five were left; these five joined Kadmos and became the founders of the five great families of Thebes.

Kadmos's city rapidly became rich and powerful, and its founder prospered with it. He married Harmonia, the daughter of Ares and Aphrodite, and they had four daughters, Ino, Autonoe, Agave and Semele, and one son, Polydoros. These in turn produced children of their own. Autonoe was the mother of Aktaion, the great hunter torn to death by his own hounds after Artemis had turned him into a stag as a punishment for seeing her naked.

Kadmos and the Serpent *Kadmos (left) advances on the rearing Serpent with drawn sword; among those watching him are the goddess Athena and the personification of his future city of Thebes. Athenian red-figured hydria (water-jar), about 430–410 BC.*

The beautiful Semele was seduced by Zeus and became pregnant with his child, the wine-god Dionysos. Zeus's divine wife Hera was jealous and cleverly suggested to Semele that she should ask Zeus to appear to her in the form in which he appeared to Hera. Because Semele had made Zeus promise to grant any request she made, he was obliged to reveal himself as a flash of lightning, which burnt her alive. Zeus snatched the child from her womb and implanted him in his own thigh, from which he was in due time born.

Semele's family refused to believe that Zeus was responsible for their sister's condition, or her death. And as the worship of Dionysos spread throughout Greece, it met with much enthusiasm and little resistance save in Thebes, where Dionysos's cousin Pentheus, Agave's son, refused to accept it.

Pentheus

A major feature of the worship of Dionysos in classical times was the formation of bands of women known as maenads; these would wander for days at a time in an ecstatic trance or frenzy over the mountainsides, drinking wine, suckling young animals or tearing them to pieces and eating them, charming snakes and generally running wild. Because of this orgiastic aspect and because its devotees were principally women, the worship of Dionysos was regarded with suspicion by the male authorities who liked to keep women in the house and under their control. Euripides's tragedy *The Bacchai* depicts an extreme case of Dionysiac revelry and male suspicion. In the play Dionysos himself comes to Thebes, determined to punish his mother's family for their lack of faith in both their sister and himself. The women of Thebes, including Semele's sisters, are all carried away by enthusiasm for the god; caught up in the revelry, they roam wild on Mount Kithairon for much of the play. Pentheus, the ruler of Thebes, regards his long-haired, effeminate cousin Dionysos with considerable suspicion, but as the god gradually drives him mad, he is brought to confess his desire to go out on to the mountain and spy upon the maenads. So Dionysos takes him up there, and when they come upon the women, the god bends down a tall pine tree so that Pentheus can perch on the top and see as much as he wants. Predictably he becomes an easy target for the maenads, who uproot the tree and tear him to pieces with their bare hands. Foremost among them is Pentheus's own mother, Agave, who returns triumphantly to Thebes bearing her son's head, believing it to be the head of a young lion. As the play ends, she is brought to realise what she has done, and all admit the power of the god.

The House of Oedipus

Oedipus, the great-great grandson of Kadmos, is today perhaps the best known of the Greek heroes after Herakles; he is famous for solving the riddle of the Sphinx, but still more notorious for his incestuous relationship with his mother. In ancient Greece he was renowned for both these episodes, but he was also more generally significant as the archetypical tragic hero, whose history embodied the universal human predicament of ignorance – man's lack of understanding of who he is and his blindness in the face of destiny.

Oedipus was born in Thebes, the son of Laios, its king, and his wife Jocasta. Because an oracle foretold that Laios would meet his death at the hands of his son, the infant Oedipus was given to a shepherd to expose on Mount Kithairon, his ankles pierced so that he could not crawl away. This was the origin of his name, which means 'swollen foot'. However, the kindly shepherd could not bring himself to abandon the child, and so handed him to another shepherd from the opposite side of the mountain. This shepherd in turn brought the child to Polybus, king of Corinth, who, being childless, was glad to raise the boy as his own. While Oedipus was growing up, he was taunted by remarks to the effect that he was not Polybus's own son; although Polybus assured him that he was, Oedipus at last resolved to travel to Delphi and consult the oracle. The oracle did not reveal his true parentage, but it did tell him that he was destined to murder his father and marry his mother. Utterly horrified, and so shocked that he completely forgot his own doubts about his parentage, he left Delphi resolved never to return to Corinth while Polybus and his wife were alive.

Unknown to Oedipus, his real father Laios was also travelling in the neighbourhood of Delphi. At a place where three roads met Oedipus came alongside Laios's chariot; a member of Laios's escort roughly ordered Oedipus out of the way, and he, in no mood to comply, lashed out. As the chariot passed, Laios himself struck Oedipus with a staff and Oedipus retaliated by dragging him out of the chariot and killing him. He then put the incident out of his mind and continued on his way.

Turning his back on Corinth, he eventually arrived at Laios's city of Thebes, which was being terrorised by the Sphinx, a monster part-winged lion, part-woman, who asked a puzzling question: 'What is it that walks upon four legs, two legs and three legs?' Those who tried and failed to solve the riddle she cast over a precipice, the foot of which was thickly littered with the bones of her victims. When the death of Laios became known in Thebes, the kingship and the hand of Laios's queen were offered to the man who could solve the riddle and free the land from the pestilent Sphinx. To Oedipus the riddle posed no problem; he was quick to identify its subject as man, who as a baby crawls upon all fours, in his prime walks upright on two legs and in old age needs the support of a third leg, a walking-stick. When the Sphinx heard his reply, she was so enraged and mortified that she flung herself from the precipice to her doom.

The citizens of Thebes received Oedipus with rapture and made him their king; he married Jocasta and for many years they lived in perfect happiness and harmony. Oedipus proved a wise and benevolent ruler, and Jocasta bore him two sons, Eteokles and Polyneikes, and two daughters, Antigone and Ismene. Eventually, however, another plague came over the land of Thebes, and it is at this point in the story that Sophocles's great tragedy

Oedipus and the Sphinx *Oedipus sits on his mantle gesturing conversationally towards the Sphinx, who sits bolt upright on a rock in front of him. Athenian red-figured hydria (water-jar), about 380–360* BC, *in the collection of Sigmund Freud.*

Oedipus Tyrannos begins. The crops are dying in the fields and orchards, the animals are barren, children falling sick and unborn babies withering in their mothers' wombs, while the gods are deaf to all appeals. Jocasta's brother Kreon returns from consulting the Delphic oracle, which ordains that the pollution will be lifted only when the killer of Laios is brought to justice. Oedipus immediately and energetically undertakes to seek him out, and as a first step consults the blind prophet Teiresias. Teiresias is reluctant to reveal the identity of the killer, but is gradually goaded to fury by Oedipus's insinuations that he himself must have had something to do with the murder. Eventually he announces that Oedipus himself is the sinner who has brought pollution upon the city; he also prophesies that Oedipus, who thinks himself so wise and so far-sighted, will refuse to accept the truth of his words, refuse to recognise who he is or what he has done.

Oedipus, enraged, suspects that his brother-in-law Kreon is plotting with Teiresias to take over the throne; nor can Kreon say anything to reassure him. Jocasta tries to smooth things over: it is impossible that Oedipus killed Laios, she says, for Laios was killed at a place where three roads meet. Suddenly Oedipus remembers his chance encounter with the old man near Delphi; questioning Jocasta about Laios's appearance (oddly enough, he looked rather like Oedipus himself) and the number of his escort, he realises that Laios was probably his victim. As he waits for confirmation to arrive from the one member of the escort who returned to Thebes, a messenger arrives from Corinth with the reassuring news that Polybus has died a natural death; Oedipus, not yet suspecting the full extent of his crime, is thankful that he seems to have evaded at least part of the oracle, but resolves to be cautious still lest he find himself marrying his mother.

The well-meaning messenger, anxious to put his mind at rest, assures him that Polybus and his wife were not his real parents; the messenger himself had received Oedipus, when a baby, from one of Laios's shepherds on Mount Kithairon, and given him to Polybus. Even now Oedipus fails to make the proper connection, and while the terrified Jocasta tries in vain to persuade him to halt his investigation, he persists in his efforts to get to the bottom of the mystery and demands that Laios's shepherd, now an old man, be brought before him. By a trick of fate this man is also the sole surviving witness to the murder of Laios. When he finally appears, the full horror of the situation is at last brought home to Oedipus; the man admits that he took Laios's son and out of pity gave him to Polybus's shepherd instead of leaving him to die. This child was Oedipus, who has now succeeded to his father's throne and bed.

Jocasta has not waited for the dénouement; she has gone ahead of Oedipus into the palace, and when he follows her with what seems like murderous intent, he finds that she has hanged herself. Tearing the golden brooches from her dress, he plunges them again and again into his eyes until blood runs down his face in streams. How can he bear to look upon the world, now that he sees the truth? The chorus in the play is left to point the moral of the story: however secure a man may feel, however rich, powerful and outwardly fortunate he may appear, no one can be confident of escaping disaster; it is not safe to call anyone happy this side of the grave.

Although he begged Kreon for immediate banishment, Oedipus was not allowed to leave Thebes for several years, until this punishment had been ratified by an oracle. By the time he was sent away, he was much less anxious to go. Now an old man, he was condemned to wander from place to place begging for food and refuge, his blind footsteps guided by his daughters Antigone and Ismene. While they brought him comfort and even some happiness, his sons, Polyneikes and Eteokles, were increasingly estranged from him, from their uncle Kreon and from each other. It had been arranged that they would take it in turns to rule for a year at a time, but when Eteokles's first year was up he refused to hand over the throne to his brother. Polyneikes took refuge in Argos, where he gathered around him a band of six other champions with whom he proposed to lay siege to his native city. Such is the state of affairs at the beginning of Sophocles's *Oedipus at Colonos*, when Oedipus, drawing near to the end of his life, arrives in the olive groves of Colonos, a district on the outskirts of Athens.

Supported by Antigone, Oedipus takes refuge at an altar to await the arrival of Theseus, king of Athens, when Ismene arrives with news from Thebes. The rival factions of the brothers are growing daily more heated, and an oracle has pronounced that the side which can gain possession of Oedipus will emerge the winner. Oedipus, equally irritated with Kreon and both his sons, is adamant that he will not support either side; they can fight it out between themselves, and he hopes that they will destroy each other in the process. When Theseus arrives, therefore, Oedipus asks to be allowed to end his days in Athens. Theseus listens with favour to his request and offers to take Oedipus somewhere more comfortable, but Oedipus wishes to remain where he is. Then Kreon appears, determined to get Oedipus to accompany him back not to Thebes, but to the city's frontier, so that while avoiding the pollution of having Oedipus actually on Theban soil, his faction might be protected by his close proximity. When Oedipus spurns Kreon's pretence at friendship and rejects his offer out of hand, Kreon becomes violent and threatens to take Oedipus by force; he has already captured Ismene, and now his soldiers drag Antigone too away from her helpless father.

Theseus, returning just in time to stop Oedipus being dragged from the altar, is highly critical of Kreon's actions and promises to restore Oedipus's daughters to him; he orders Kreon back to Thebes. Polyneikes then arrives, also with a political reason for desiring the protection of the father whom he helped eject from Thebes; he too is sent packing, as Oedipus announces his intention of remaining at Colonos to the end of his days. The play ends dramatically: after Oedipus disappears into the sacred grove, a messenger emerges to recount his miraculous end, witnessed only by Theseus. Oedipus, it is pronounced, has transferred the blessings he could have given Kreon or Polyneikes to Athens, which will hereafter be protected by his presence.

The attack made on Thebes by Polyneikes and his allies is the subject of Aeschylus's *Seven Against Thebes*. Seven champions lead the attack at the seven gates of Thebes, and it falls to Polyneikes to take the gate defended by his brother Eteokles. Although the Thebans finally repulse the attack upon their city, the two brothers die by each other's swords, thus fulfilling their father's curse and continuing the unhappy saga of the house of Oedipus.

The dramatic action of Sophocles's *Antigone* begins at this point in the story. With Oedipus's male heirs both dead, Kreon assumes the title of king of Thebes. He decrees that while Eteokles should be buried with all ceremony, the traitor Polyneikes must be left where he fell, to have his corpse destroyed by dogs and birds of prey. Kreon sets a guard over the corpse to ensure that his edict is obeyed, and soon his soldiers return with Antigone, who has been caught throwing handfuls of soil over her brother's mangled remains in an effort to provide him with a symbolic burial. When challenged with her disobedience, she replies that the laws of the gods, which require that kinsmen be buried, are irrevocable and immutable and must take precedence over the laws of man. In his *Antigone*, Sophocles uses the myth to explore this conflict between human and divine law: what is the ordinary person supposed to do when the two sets of laws conflict? Although ultimately the answer seems to be that the divine law must be obeyed at whatever cost, the issue is by no means clear-cut from the start. While Antigone is portrayed as a headstrong, unfeminine woman who is not content to remain in the traditional female realm of the home but ventures out to defy the laws of her male guardian, Kreon comes across initially as a man doing his best to govern his city by the rule of law.

When Antigone shows no remorse for her crime, Kreon orders her to be entombed alive, a cruel method of execution calculated to absolve him from direct responsibility for her death. At this point Antigone's fiancé, Kreon's son Haimon, comes to Kreon to plead for her life, pointing out that the punishment is both barbarous and politically unwise, for Antigone is well on the way to becoming a heroine among the people of Thebes. Kreon, however, remains obdurate, like the trees that will not bend to the torrent on the margins of a flooded river, or the sailor who will not slacken his sheets before the gale; and so he gives instructions for the entombment to go ahead. Only when the prophet Teiresias appears, and reveals the anger of the gods and the terrible punishment that will fall upon Kreon if he persists in this course of action, does Kreon at last take the advice of the chorus and set off to release Antigone from her prison. Foolishly, as it turns out, he stops on the way to bury the remains of Eteokles and only arrives at the tomb to find Haimon holding the body of Antigone – she has hanged herself with her girdle. Haimon then turns his sword upon himself. Kreon returns home to the news that his wife Eurydice has killed herself, too, cursing her husband with her dying breath. Utterly crushed by the tragedy that has so suddenly befallen him, Kreon is led away, and the chorus is left to reflect that the greater part of happiness is wisdom, coupled with due reverence for the gods.

The imaginative legacy

There would have been no market for a book on myths in fifth-century Athens, since the Greeks did not relegate them to a separate section of their lives. The characters and episodes of mythology were, rather, integrated into Greek society, reflected in all social activities from the cradle to the grave. To ask whether the average fifth-century Athenian 'believed' in all these stories is probably anachronistic. If the question is about accepting them as historical fact, it becomes part of a larger discussion of how the Greeks saw history, while if we are equating 'belief' with 'religious faith', a similar problem of definition arises.

The surviving evidence suggests that mythology was a natural and accepted part of life, which operated simultaneously on several different levels. The stories provided popular entertainment, their expression inspiring those excursions into music, poetry and the visual arts for which the Greek world is justly famous. At the same time, myths provided an inexhaustible stock of examples, not merely of good and bad behaviour for instructing the young, but also of the workings of fate, destiny and character, and the mystery of life, for older people to ponder. Moreover, the complex patterns of mythology, the functions and interrelationships of gods and heroes and their associations with particular places, formed the basis of the intricate network of cults whose observance was so important to the Greek social structure.

All civilisations need mythologies, and many invent their own. But because Greek civilisation is the foundation of Western society, and the study of Greek culture has been so important in the education systems of the Western world until relatively recently, many Western societies have adopted Greek myths and used them alongside their own contemporary or historic legends. The Romans led the way, adapting the Greek pantheon only very slightly in order to accommodate a few local Italic deities, and endlessly reproducing Greek myths in their literature and their art. For Romans of both the Republic and the Empire, Greece represented culture and civilisation; those who wished to demonstrate their taste and erudition decorated the walls of their houses with paintings of Greek myths, and after they died they had themselves placed in marble coffins bearing sculptured panels depicting the battles of the Greeks and the Amazons, or the wine-god Dionysos with his entourage. The subject matter of Roman poetry, too, was basically Greek; many Greek myths are preserved only thanks to the Augustan poet Ovid, while his contemporary Virgil legitimised and glorified the origins and growth of Rome in his epic poem of the *Aeneid*, whose story starts in the Sack of Troy, the greatest of all Greek myths.

The widespread adoption of Christianity did nothing to curb the popularity of the characters and stories of the myths and their continual recycling in art, music and literature. With the rediscovery of classical antiquity in the Renaissance, the poetry of Ovid became a major influence on the imagination of poets and artists. His were among the first classical texts to benefit from the invention of printing in the late fifteenth century; they were widely and enthusiastically translated, and remained a fundamental influence on the diffusion and perception of Greek myths through subsequent centuries. From the early years of the Renaissance, artists were happy to portray the pagan subjects of Greek mythology alongside more conventional Christian themes: so today in the Uffizi Gallery in Florence, Botticelli's 'Birth of Venus' or 'Pallas and the Centaur' rub shoulders with the same artist's Annunciations and Madonnas. Italy, and Rome in particular, became an important focus for artists interested in the classical past, from the early Renaissance until well into the eighteenth century. Artists of all nationalities were attracted there, including, in the seventeenth century, the Frenchmen Nicolas Poussin and Claude Lorrain; for them the classical world provided as much inspiration as the Christian, the two traditions happily fused in Rome.

In northern Europe, classical mythology never took the same hold of the visual arts, but its effect was very obvious in literature: in Elizabethan England, for example, classical texts both Latin and Greek were translated with enthusiasm, so that the stories of mythology became easily available to contemporary poets. In seventeenth-century France, too, Greek tragedy found contemporary relevance at the hands of such masters as Racine, who reworked the ancient myths – including those of Phaidra, Andromache, Oedipus and Iphigeneia – to new purpose.

The eighteenth century saw the philosophical revolution of the Enlightenment spread throughout Europe, accompanied by a certain reaction against Greek myth. In this age of reason some poured scorn on the frivolous nature of the myths, and there was a tendency to dwell rather on the scientific and philosophical achievements of Greece and Rome; typical of this attitude is Jacques-Louis David's painting of the 'Death of Socrates'. It was, however, impossible for the myths to be entirely overlooked, and they continued to provide an important source of raw material for dramatists, including those who wrote the libretti for Handel's operas *Admeto* and *Semele*, Mozart's *Idomeneo* and Gluck's *Iphigénie en Aulide*.

By the end of the century, Romanticism was regaining the upper hand, and there was an enormous surge of enthusiasm for all things Greek. This was partly because Greece was joining Italy as an important destination on the Grand Tour. The more practical among the wealthy youth of Europe who had visited the shores of the Aegean, such as the architects James ('Athenian') Stuart and Nicholas Revett, returned home to recreate in northern landscapes the proportions and styles of the ruined buildings they had seen.

The more imaginative would revisit in their mind's eye the scenes they had left and then re-invent the classical past itself in the great new surge of 'Greek' literature and art.

In Britain at least, the popularity of Greek myth reached its climax in the nineteenth century. It was a great period for new translations of Greek tragedies and of Homer, and these in turn inspired contemporary poets. Keats, Byron and Shelley were all indebted to the classics; indeed, it is hard to think of a nineteenth-century poet who was not. The Hellenism of Queen Victoria's poet laureate, Alfred Lord Tennyson, was such that even his portraits of the quintessentially English court of King Arthur are suffused with echoes of the Homeric epics. Several of his poems were directly inspired by classical mythology, such as his 'Lotos Eaters' – a deeply romantic vision, at once exotic and deeply depressing, of an episode touched upon very briefly in the *Odyssey*; his Odysseus (in *Ulysses*) is a strange mixture of Greek hero and restless Victorian gentleman. The visual arts kept pace, stimulated to new 'Greek' heights by the purchase for the nation of the Elgin marbles in 1816; today, many of the 'Greek' paintings of such artists as Lord Leighton or Lawrence Alma-Tadema seem comically romantic, but in their time they were seriously accepted as part of the transmission of the Hellenic ideal.

The comfortable Victorian vision of Hellenism was shattered by the First World War. Many of the young men who sailed through the Dardanelles to die at Gallipoli saw themselves, or were seen by their friends, as reincarnations of the Greek heroes who fought and died at Troy. But in the end the War broke this illusion; as one survivor, Ronald Knox, wrote later:

> The great god Pan is dead, and the world of which he is the symbol; we can never recapture it. And I knew that when I saw the Hellespont. It did not remind me of the ship *Argo*, nor of the agony of Troy ... It was peopled for me instead by those who fought and died there fifteen years ago, men of my own country and of my own speech.

However, Western Europe's interest in Greek mythology did not altogether die in 1918. One of the most intriguing twentieth-century obsessions with Greek mythology is that of Sigmund Freud, the father of psychoanalysis. Greek myths, along with other aspects of the classical past, were intensely important to Freud, who recognised that they embodied universal human themes. He saw in them both anticipation and confirmation of his theories, and his published writings are full of allusions to the myths. He compared, for example, his technique of extracting the supposedly indestructible unconscious wishes of his patients to the way in which Odysseus induced the ghosts he met in the Underworld to speak by letting them drink the sacrificial blood. It was Freud who made Oedipus a household name by calling after him a complex that he claimed to have identified in the majority of little boys, their tendency to fall deeply in love with their mothers and consequently to become intensely jealous of their fathers. Freud certainly believed this had happened to him, and in other respects, too, he identified himself with Oedipus, the solver of riddles. He was a passionate collector of Greek, Roman and Egyptian

Captive Andromache, by Frederic Leighton *(above) The wife of Hector was condemned to slavery by the fall of Troy; here she stands, isolated and tragic, at the fountain. About 1888.*

Electra at the tomb of Agamemnon, by Frederic Leighton *(left) Standing beside her father's tomb, Electra's demeanour is despairing, her grief emphasised by the darkness of her clothing. About 1869.*

Terracotta Sphinx *(below) This is from the ancient art collection of Sigmund Freud, who was fascinated by the Oedipus legend. South-Italian Greek, about 400 BC.*

antiquities, and his friends and patients seem to have lost no opportunity of presenting him with any representation of Oedipus or the Sphinx that they could find. On his fiftieth birthday Freud's colleagues presented him with a medallion bearing his own portrait on one side and Oedipus and the Sphinx on the other, along with a line from Sophocles's *Oedipus Tyrannos*: 'he who solved the famous riddle, and was most powerful of men'.

Throughout the twentieth century Greek myths have continued to inspire poets and writers. In 1922, for example, James Joyce published *Ulysses*, a modern epic which compresses Odysseus's ten-year homeward journey to Ithaca into one day in the life of an Irish Jew in Dublin; here Aiolos, king of the Winds, becomes a newspaper editor controlling the currents of popular opinion, the Sirens are a pair of barmaids, and Circe, who turned men into swine, is the madam of a brothel. Greek myths were also important to T. S. Eliot: the central figure of *The Waste Land*, for example, is the blind Theban prophet Teiresias. Translations and adaptations, too, have flourished. In 1944 a new version of Sophocles's *Antigone* by the French dramatist Jean Anouilh showed that its central theme, of individual conscience versus the law of the state, could be of immediate and compelling relevance to contemporary political situations. But surely the most poetic of all translations is W. B. Yeats's free adaptation of the opening chorus of Sophocles's *Oedipus at Colonos*. The third stanza is an outstandingly vivid and beautiful evocation of the story of Demeter and Persephone, the myth with which this survey began:

> Who comes into this country, and has come
> Where golden crocus and narcissus bloom,
> Where the Great Mother, mourning for her daughter
> And beauty-drunken by the water
> Glittering among grey-leaved olive trees,
> Has plucked a flower and sung her loss;
> Who finds abounding Cephisus
> Has found the loveliest spectacle there is.

Even at the end of the twentieth century, Greek myths retain their appeal. Although the old stories may appear in strange new guises – Herakles is today's Superman, the modern Odyssey is the voyage of the starship *Enterprise* in 'Startrek' – the fact that they continue to be reworked shows the enduring strength of their imaginative legacy.

Suggestions for further reading

The most direct and also the most enjoyable way to approach Greek myths is to read them as they were told by the Greeks and the Romans themselves. Most Greek and Latin literature is available in translation. The Loeb Classical Library offers parallel texts in the original language and in English. Many of the translations were written some time ago, and their language is at times archaic; they are still, however, very useful to anyone with a little Greek or Latin who wishes to know from time to time what the original version says. For most people, the Penguin Classics offer a cheaper and more up-to-date alternative. They cover most of the important texts and are easy to obtain, carry around and read. They vary in style, and the translations of the *Iliad* and the *Odyssey* are generally reckoned to be more successful than those of the Greek tragedies. Rather more poetic translations of these are offered by D. Grene and R. Lattimore in *The Complete Greek Tragedies* (Chicago, 1959). Apart from the *Iliad*, the *Odyssey* and the tragedies, the most important ancient source for Greek myths is probably Ovid's *Metamorphoses*, the most easily accessible translation of which is again the Loeb edition. Greek myths may also be approached via Greek art; a valuable guide here is T. H. Carpenter's *Art and Myth in Ancient Greece* (London, 1989).

There are several dictionaries of Greek mythology. The *Oxford Classical Dictionary* (3rd edn, Oxford, 1999) provides short entries on mythological characters, alongside ancient authors and characters of history. Less dry, however, and a great deal more informative is P. Grimal's *The Dictionary of Classical Mythology* (English translation, Oxford, 1986), which provides detailed accounts of all major and minor myths, a series of useful family trees and numerous well-chosen illustrations. The *Lexicon Iconographicum Mythologiae Classicae* (*LIMC*), produced by a massive international team of art historians and archaeologists, collects together all known artistic representations of all the characters of Greek and Roman mythology; it also summarises literary sources.

A great many general books, designed to appeal to various age groups, tell the stories of Greek myths; these can be found in any bookshop or library and selection amongst them is a matter of personal preference. In the interpretation of myth, the French currently lead the field: good introductions to current ways of thinking may be found in two recent collections of essays: R. L. Gordon (ed.), *Myth, Religion and Society* (Cambridge, 1981) and J. Bremmer (ed.), *Interpretations of Greek Mythology* (London, 1988); see also R. Buxton, *From Myth to Reason* (Oxford, 2001). For a stimulating introduction to women's role in myth, see M. Lefkowicz, *Women in Greek Myth* (Bristol Classical Press, 1995).

Index and picture credits

Picture credits

Front cover: British Museum GR 1843. 11–3. 31 (Vase E440); *p. 9*: BM GR 1873. 8–20. 375 (Vase E140); *p. 12: (top left)* BM GR 1836. 2–24. 66 (Vase B248); *(top right)* Providence, R.I. 25. 078; *(bottom)* BM GR 1864. 10–7. 77 (Vase D2); *p. 13*: BM GR 1867. 5–8. 962 (Vase B424); *p. 14*: BM GR 1843. 11–3. 87 (Vase E256); *p. 15: (left)* BM GR 1980. 10–19. 1; *(right)* BM GR 1843. 11–3. 60 (Vase B215); *p. 17: (top)* BM GR 1890. 2–10. 1 (Vase F149); *(bottom)* BM GR 1814. 7–4. 2867 (Bronze 544); *p. 18*: BM GR 1843. 11–3. 63 (Vase B213); *p. 19*: BM GR 1843. 11–3. 40 (Vase B163); *p. 20: (left)* BM GR 1865. 7–12. 19–21 (Bronze 642); *(right)* BM GR 1814. 7–4. 1652; *p. 21*: BM GR 1836. 2–24. 103 (Vase B194); *p. 22: (top)* Paris, Louvre E701 (Photo M. Chuzeville); *(bottom)* BM GR 1772. 3–20. 30* (Vase E224); *p. 23: (top)* BM GR 1843. 11–3. 9 (Vase E38); *(bottom left)* BM CM BMC *Alexandria* 1054; *(bottom right)* BM GR 1842. 8. 22. 1 (Vase E458); *p. 26*: BM GR 1893. 6–28. 5 (Terracotta D594); *p. 28*: BM GR 1850. 3–2. 3 (Vase E84); *p. 29*: BM Parthenon South Metope 27; *p. 32: (top)* BM GR 1843. 11–3. 60 (Vase B215); *(bottom)* Karlsruhe, Badisches Landesmuseum 259; *p. 36*: BM GR 1846. 9–25. 3 (Vase F157); *p. 37*: New York, The Metropolitan Museum of Art 31. 11. 13. Rogers Fund, 1931; *p. 39: (top)* BM GR 1836. 2–24. 127 (Vase B210); *(bottom)* Mykonos Museum 70 (photo: DAI Athen); *p. 42*: Boston, Museum of Fine Arts 63. 1246. William Francis Warden Fund; *p. 44: (right)* Eleusis Museum 544 (photo: DAI Athen); *(left)* BM GR 1837. 6–9. 72 (Vase B687); *p. 45*: BM GR 1860. 12–1. 2 (Vase E804); *p. 47*: Boston 99. 515. H. L. Pierce Fund; *p. 49*: BM GR 1897. 7–26. 7 (Bronze 882); *pp. 53, 56*: Chiusi, Museo Archeologico 1831 (after A. Furtwängler and K. Reichhold, *Griechische Vasenmalerei*, Munich 1904–32, pl. 142); *p. 60*: BM GR 1805. 7–3. 301 (Terracotta D603); *p. 62*: BM GR 1843. 11–3. 76 (Vase E163); *p. 64: (top)* Boston 13. 200. Francis Bartlett Fund; *(bottom)* BM GR 1849. 6–20. 5 (Vase B471); *p. 65*: BM GR 1843. 11–3. 24 (Vase E169); *p. 67*: ex-Berlin, Staatliche Museen (Antikensammlung) 2634; *p. 70*: London, Freud Museum 3117; *p. 77: (above)* Manchester City Art Galleries; *(bottom left)* Ferens Art Gallery: Hull City Museums and Art Galleries (UK); *(bottom right)* Freud Museum 4387.